MW00592641

HISTORY & GEOGRAPHY 900
Teacher's Guide

Author:
Teresa Busky, B.A., J.D.

Editor:
Alan Christopherson, M.S.

804 N. 2nd Ave. E.
Rock Rapids, IA 51246-1759

© MCMXCVI by Alpha Omega Publications, Inc. All rights reserved.
LIFEPAC is a registered trademark of Alpha Omega Publications, Inc.

All trademarks and/or service marks referenced in this material are the property of their respective owners.
Alpha Omega Publications, Inc. makes no claim of ownership to any trademarks and/or service marks other
than their own and their affiliates', and makes no claim of affiliation to any companies whose trademarks
may be listed in this material, other than their own.

HISTORY & GEOGRAPHY 900

LIFEPAC® Overview

HISTORY & GEOGRAPHY SCOPE & SEQUENCE

	Your World (Grade 1)	U.S. History (Grade 2)	U.S. Geography and History (Grade 3)
Unit 1	I AM A SPECIAL PERSON • God made me • You are God's child • All about you • Using proper manners	LOOKING BACK Remembering last year Learning about early times The trail of the Native Americans Symbols and historic places	U.S. GEOGRAPHY AND HISTORY STUDY SKILLS • Map skills • Resources • Community
Unit 2	LET'S COMMUNICATE • Sounds people make • Sounds that communicate • Communicating without sound • Communicating with God	SETTLING THE NEW WORLD The first settlers Colonies of the new world War for Independence Symbols and historical places	NEW ENGLAND STATES • ME, NH, VT, MA, RI, and CT • New England geography • New England resources • New England community
Unit 3	I HAVE FEELINGS • I feel sad • I feel afraid • I feel happy • I have other feelings	A NEW GOVERNMENT FOR A NEW COUNTRY A study of government Creating a government Our government Symbols and historical places	MID-ATLANTIC STATES • NY, PA, NJ, DE, MD, and DC • Mid-Atlantic geography • Mid-Atlantic resources • Mid-Atlantic community
Unit 4	I LIVE IN A FAMILY • My mother and father • My brothers and sisters • My grandparents • What my family does	GOVERNMENT UNDER THE CONSTITUTION Article One -- The Legislative Branch Article Two -- The Executive Branch Article Three -- The Judicial Branch The Bill of Rights -- Symbols and historical places	SOUTHERN-ATLANTIC STATES • WV, VA, NC, SC, GA, and FL • Southern Atlantic geography • Southern Atlantic resources • Southern Atlantic community
Unit 5	YOU BELONG TO FAMILIES • Getting ready in the morning • Walking to school • The school family • The church family	OUR GOVERNMENT CLOSE TO HOME Our state governments Our local governments Citizens of the United States Symbols and historical places	SOUTHERN STATES • KY, TN, MS, LA, AL, OK, TX, and AR • Southern geography • Southern resources • Southern community
Unit 6	PLACES PEOPLE LIVE • Life on the farm • Life in the city • Life by the sea	WESTWARD -- FROM THE ORIGINAL COLONIES The United States grows The Lewis and Clark Expedition The Old Southwest Symbols and historical places	GREAT LAKES STATES • OH, IN, IL, MI, WI, and MN • Great Lakes geography • Great Lakes resources • Great Lakes community
Unit 7	COMMUNITY HELPERS • Firefighters and police officers • Doctors • City workers • Teachers and ministers	SETTLING THE FRONTIER The Texas frontier Westward expansion Meet America's pioneers Symbols and historical places	MIDWESTERN STATES • ND, SD, NE, KS, MO, and IA • Midwestern geography • Midwestern resources • Midwestern community
Unit 8	I LOVE MY COUNTRY • America discovered • The Pilgrims • The United States begins • Respect for your country	EXPLORING AMERICA WITH MAPS Directions on a map Reading roads and symbols Natural features Symbols and historical places	MOUNTAIN STATES • MT, ID, WY, NV, UT, CO, AZ, and NM • Mountain geography • Mountain resources • Mountain community
Unit 9	I LIVE IN THE WORLD • The globe • Countries • Friends in Mexico • Friends in Japan	PAST, PRESENT, AND FUTURE MAPS City maps Building maps History of maps Symbols and historical places	PACIFIC STATES • WA, OR, CA, AK, and HI • Pacific geography • Pacific resources • Pacific community
Unit 10	THE WORLD AND YOU • You are special • Your family • Your school and church • Your world	REVIEW UNITED STATES HISTORY The United States begins Creating a government Mapping the United States	U.S. GEOGRAPHY AND HISTORY REVIEW • U.S. geographical features • Eastern U.S. review • Western U.S. review

HISTORY & GEOGRAPHY SCOPE & SEQUENCE

World Geography and Culture (Grade 4)	U.S. History (Grade 5)	Civilizations (Grade 6)	
OUR EARTH • The surface of the Earth • Early explorations of the Earth • Exploring from space • Exploring the oceans	**A NEW WORLD** • Exploration of America • The first colonies • Conflict with Britain • Birth of the United States	**WORLD GEOGRAPHY** • Latitude and longitude • Western and eastern hemispheres • The southern hemisphere • Political and cultural regions	Unit 1
SEAPORT CITIES • Sydney • Hong Kong • Istanbul • London	**A NEW NATION** • War for Independence • Life in America • A new form of government • The nation's early years	**THE CRADLE OF CIVILIZATION** • Mesopotamia • The land of Israel • The nation of Israel • Egypt	Unit 2
DESERT LANDS • What is a desert? • Where are the deserts? • How do people live in the desert?	**A TIME OF TESTING** • Louisiana Purchase • War of 1812 • Sectionalism • Improvements in trade and travel	**THE CIVILIZATIONS OF GREECE AND ROME** • Geography of the region • Beginning civilizations • Contributions to other civilizations • The influence of Christianity	Unit 3
GRASSLANDS • Grasslands of the world • Ukraine • Kenya • Argentina	**A GROWING NATION** • Andrew Jackson's influence • Texas and Oregon • Mexican War • The nation divides	**LIFE IN THE MIDDLE AGES** • The feudal system • Books and schools • The Crusades • Trade and architecture	Unit 4
TROPICAL RAINFORESTS • Facts about rainforests • Rainforests of the world • The Amazon rainforest • The Congo rainforest	**A DIVIDED NATION** • Civil War • Reconstruction • Gilded Age • The need for reform	**SIX SOUTH AMERICAN COUNTRIES** • Brazil • Colombia • Venezuela • Three Guianas	Unit 5
THE POLAR REGIONS • The polar regions: coldest places in the world • The Arctic polar region • The Antarctic polar region	**A CHANGING NATION** • Progressive reforms • Spanish-American War • World War I • Roaring Twenties	**OTHER SOUTH AMERICAN COUNTRIES** • Ecuador and Peru • Bolivia and Uruguay • Paraguay and Argentina • Chile	Unit 6
MOUNTAIN COUNTRIES • Peru — the Andes • The Incas and modern Peru • Nepal — the Himalayas • Switzerland — the Alps	**DEPRESSION AND WAR** • The Great Depression • War begins in Europe • War in Europe • War in the Pacific	**AFRICA** • Geography and cultures • Countries of northern Africa • Countries of central Africa • Countries of southern Africa	Unit 7
ISLAND COUNTRIES • Islands of the Earth • Cuba • Iceland • Japan	**COLD WAR** • Korean War and other crises • Vietnam War • Civil Rights movement • Upheaval in America	**MODERN WESTERN EUROPE** • The Renaissance • The Industrial Revolution • World War I • World War II	Unit 8
NORTH AMERICA • Geography • Lands, lakes, and rivers • Northern countries • Southern countries	**INTO THE NEW MILLENNIUM** • Watergate and détente • The fall of communism • The Persian Gulf • Issues of the new millennium	**MODERN EASTERN EUROPE** • Early government • Early churches • Early countries • Modern countries	Unit 9
OUR WORLD IN REVIEW • Europe and the explorers • Asia and Africa • Southern continents • North America and the North Pole	**THE UNITED STATES OF AMERICA** • Beginning America until 1830 • Stronger America 1830-1930 • 1930 to the end of the millennium • The new millennium	**DEVELOPMENT OF OUR WORLD** • Cradle of civilization • The Middle Ages • Modern Europe • South America and Africa	Unit 10

HISTORY & GEOGRAPHY SCOPE & SEQUENCE

	Anthropology, Sociology, Economics, and State History (Grade 7)	U.S. History (Grade 8)	Civics and World Geography (Grade 9)
Unit 1	WHAT IS HISTORY? • Definition and significance of history • Historians and the historical method • Views of history	EUROPE COMES TO AMERICA • Voyages of Columbus • Spanish exploration • Other exploration • The first colonies	HERITAGE OF THE UNITED STATES • American colonies • Acquisitions and annexations • Backgrounds to freedom • Backgrounds to society
Unit 2	WHAT IS GEOGRAPHY? • Classes of geography • Geography and relief of the Earth • Maps and the study of our world • Time zones	BRITISH AMERICA • English colonies • Government • Lifestyle • Wars with France	OUR NATIONAL GOVERNMENT • Ideals of national government • National government developed • Legislative and executive branches • Judicial branch
Unit 3	U.S. HISTORY AND GEOGRAPHY • Geography of the United States • Early history of the United States • Physical regions of the United States • Cultural regions of the United States	THE AMERICAN REVOLUTION • British control • Rebellion of the colonies • War for independence • Constitution	STATE AND LOCAL GOVERNMENT • Powers of state government • County government • Township government • City government
Unit 4	ANTHROPOLOGY • Understanding anthropology • The unity of man • The diversity of man • The culture of man	A FIRM FOUNDATION • Washington's presidency • Adams' administration • Jeffersonian Democracy • War of 1812	PLANNING A CAREER • Definition of a career • God's will concerning a career • Selecting a career • Preparation for a career
Unit 5	SOCIOLOGY — MAN IN GROUPS • Sociology defined • Historical development • Importance to Christians • Method of sociology	A GROWING NATION • Jacksonian Era • Northern border • Southern border • Industrial Revolution	CITIZENSHIP • Citizenship defined • Gaining citizenship • Rights of citizenship • Responsibilities of citizenship
Unit 6	U.S. ANTHROPOLOGY AND SOCIOLOGY • Cultural background of the United States • Native American cultures • Cultures from distant lands • Cultural and social interaction	THE CIVIL WAR • Division and secession • Civil War • Death of Lincoln • Reconstruction	THE EARTH AND MAN • Man inhabits the Earth • Man's home on the Earth • Man develops the Earth • The future of the Earth
Unit 7	ECONOMICS — RESOURCES AND NEED • Economics defined • Methods of the economist • Tools of the economist • An experiment in economy	GILDED AGE TO PROGRESSIVE ERA • Rise of industry • Wild West • America as a world power • Progressive era	REGIONS OF THE WORLD • A region defined • Geographic and climate regions • Cultural and political regions • *Economic regions, European Union,*
Unit 8	POLITICAL SCIENCE • Definition of political science • Roots of Western thought • Modern political thinkers • *Political theory*	A WORLD IN CONFLICT • World War I • Great Depression • New Deal • World War II	MAN AND HIS ENVIRONMENT • The physical environment • Drug abuse, *Food Additives* • *Natural Resource Shortages* → *Man and his social environment* → *Man and his responsibilities to environ*
Unit 9	STATE ECONOMICS AND POLITICS • Background of state government • State government • State finance • State politics	COLD WAR AMERICA • Origins of the Cold War • Vietnam • Truman to Nixon • Ending of the Cold War	TOOLS OF THE GEOGRAPHER • The globe • Types of maps • Reading maps • The Earth in symbol form
Unit 10	SOCIAL SCIENCES REVIEW • History and geography • Anthropology • Sociology • Economics and politics	RECENT AMERICA AND REVIEW • Europe to independence • Colonies to the Civil War • Civil War to World War II • World War II through the Cold War	MAN IN A CHANGING WORLD • Development of the nation • Development of government • Development of the Earth • Solving problems

Handwritten annotations:

- *European Free Trade Assoc.*
- *NAFTA and USMCA, ASEAN, GATT*
- *Changes within Federal govt. Labor market problems Increasing cost of living*
- *physical conservation and restoration social betterment*
- *the Earth in model form — The Globe*
- *The Earth in Picture Form — the Map*
- *Graphs and charts*
- *Commitment to the Future*

HISTORY & GEOGRAPHY SCOPE & SEQUENCE

World History (Grade 10)	American History (Grade 11)	Government and Economics (Grade 12)	
ANCIENT CIVILIZATIONS 1 • Origin of civilization • Early Egypt • Assyria and Babylonia • Persian civilization	FOUNDATION OF THE REPUBLIC • Democracy develops • Virginia • New England colonies • Middle and southern colonies	INTERNATIONAL GOVERNMENTS • Why have governments? • Types of governments • Governments in our world • Political thinkers	Unit 1
ANCIENT CIVILIZATIONS 2 • India • China • Greek civilization • Roman Empire	DEVELOPMENT OF CONSTITUTIONAL GOVERNMENT • Relations with England • The Revolutionary War • Articles of Confederation • Constitution of the United States	UNITED STATES GOVERNMENT • U.S. Constitution • Bill of Rights • Three branches of government • Legislative process	Unit 2
THE MEDIEVAL WORLD • Early Middle Ages • Middle Ages in transition • High Middle Ages	NATIONAL EXPANSION • A strong federal government • Revolution of 1800 • War of 1812 • Nationalism and sectionalism	AMERICAN PARTY SYSTEM • American party system • Development of political parties • Functions of political parties • Voting	Unit 3
RENAISSANCE AND REFORMATION • Changes in government and art • Changes in literature and thought • Advances in science • Reform within the church	A NATION DIVIDED • Issues of division • Division of land and people • Economics of slavery • Politics of slavery	HISTORY OF GOVERNMENTS • Primitive governments • Beginnings of democracy • Feudalism, theocracy, and democracy • Fascism and Nazism	Unit 4
GROWTH OF WORLD EMPIRES • England and France • Portugal and Spain • Austria and Germany • Italy and the Ottoman Empire	A NATION DIVIDED AND UNITED • Regionalism • The division • The Civil War • Reconstruction	THE CHRISTIAN AND HIS GOVERNMENT • Discrimination and the Christian • Christian attitudes • Public opinion and truth in politics • Politics and propaganda	Unit 5
THE AGE OF REVOLUTION • Factors leading to revolution • The English Revolution • The American Revolution • The French Revolution	U.S. INVOLVEMENT AT HOME AND ABROAD • Surge of industry • The industrial lifestyle • Isolationism • Involvement in conflict	FREE ENTERPRISE • Economics • Competition • Money through history • International finance and currency	Unit 6
THE INDUSTRIAL REVOLUTION • Sparks of preparation • Industrial Revolution in England • Industrial Revolution in America • Social changes of the revolution	THE SEARCH FOR PEACE • World War I and its aftermath • The Golden Twenties • The Great Depression • The New Deal	BUSINESS AND YOU • Running a business • Government and business • Banks and mergers • Deregulation and bankruptcy	Unit 7
TWO WORLD WARS • Mounting tension • World War I • Peace and power quests • World War II	A NATION AT WAR • Causes of the war • World War II • Korean conflict • Vietnam conflict	THE STOCK MARKET • How it started and works • Selecting stocks • Types of stocks • Tracking stocks	Unit 8
THE 20TH CENTURY AFTER 1945 • The Cold War • Korean War and Vietnam War • Collapse of the Soviet Union • The 20th century closes	CONTEMPORARY AMERICA • America in the 1960s • America in the 1970s • America in the 1980s and 1990s • International scene of the 1980s to 1990s	BUDGET AND FINANCE • Cash, credit, and checking • Buying a car • Grants, loans, and IRAs • Savings and eCash	Unit 9
ANCIENT TIMES TO THE 21ST CENTURY • Ancient civilizations • Medieval times • Renaissance and Reformation • Revolutions and Globalization	UNITED STATES HISTORY • Basis of democracy • The 1800s • Industrialization • Current history	GEOGRAPHY • Euro and International finance • U.S. geography • The global traveler • Neighbors, heroes, and the Holy Land	Unit 10

STRUCTURE OF THE LIFEPAC CURRICULUM

The LIFEPAC curriculum is conveniently structured to provide one Teacher's Guide containing teacher support material with answer keys and ten student worktexts for each subject at grade levels 2 through 12. The worktext format of the LIFEPACs allows the student to read the textual information and complete workbook activities all in the same booklet. The easy-to-follow LIFEPAC numbering system lists the grade as the first number(s) and the last two digits as the number of the series. For example, the Language Arts LIFEPAC at the 6th grade level, 5th book in the series would be LAN0605.

Each LIFEPAC is divided into three to five sections and begins with an introduction or overview of the booklet as well as a series of specific learning objectives to give a purpose to the study of the LIFEPAC. The introduction and objectives are followed by a vocabulary section which may be found at the beginning of each section at the lower levels or in the glossary at the high school level. Vocabulary words are used to develop word recognition and should not be confused with the spelling words introduced later in the LIFEPAC. The student should learn all vocabulary words before working the LIFEPAC sections to improve comprehension, retention, and reading skills.

Each activity or written assignment in grades 2 through 12 has a number for easy identification, such as 1.1. The first number corresponds to the LIFEPAC section and the number to the right of the decimal is the number of the activity.

Teacher checkpoints, which are essential to maintain quality learning, are found at various locations throughout the LIFEPAC.

The teacher should check 1) neatness of work and penmanship, 2) quality of understanding (tested with a short oral quiz), 3) thoroughness of answers (complete sentences and paragraphs, correct spelling, etc.), 4) completion of activities (no blank spaces), and 5) accuracy of answers as compared to the answer key (all answers correct).

The self test questions in grades 2 through 12 are also number coded for easy reference. For example, 2.015 means that this is the 15th question in the self test of Section 2. The first number corresponds to the LIFEPAC section, the zero indicates that it is a self test question, and the number to the right of the zero the question number.

The LIFEPAC test is packaged at the center of each LIFEPAC. It should be removed and put aside before giving the booklet to the student for study.

Answer and test keys in grades 2 through 12 have the same numbering system as the LIFEPACs. The student may be given access to the answer keys (not the test keys) under teacher supervision so that they can score their own work.

A thorough study of the Scope & Sequence by the teacher before instruction begins is essential to the success of the student. The teacher should become familiar with expected skill mastery and understand how these grade-level skills fit into the overall skill development of the curriculum. The teacher should also preview the objectives that appear at the beginning of each LIFEPAC for additional preparation and planning.

TEST SCORING AND GRADING

Answer keys and test keys give examples of correct answers. They convey the idea, but the student may use many ways to express a correct answer. The teacher should check for the essence of the answer, not for the exact wording. Many questions are high level and require thinking and creativity on the part of the student. Each answer should be scored based on whether or not the main idea written by the student matches the model example. "Any Order" or "Either Order" in a key indicates that no particular order is necessary to be correct.

Most self tests and LIFEPAC tests at the lower elementary levels are scored at 1 point per answer; however, the upper levels may have a point system awarding 2 to 5 points for various answers or questions. Further, the total test points will vary; they may not always equal 100 points. They may be 78, 85, 100, 105, etc.

Example 1

Example 2

A score box similar to ex. 1 above is located at the end of each self test and on the front of the LIFEPAC test. The bottom score, 72, represents the total number of points possible on the test. The upper score, 58, represents the number of points your student will need to receive an 80% or passing grade. If you wish to establish the exact percentage that your student has achieved, find the total points of their correct answers and divide it by the bottom number (in this case 72). For example, if your student has a point total of 65, divide 65 by 72 for a grade of 90%. Referring to ex. 2, on a test with a total of 105 possible points, the student would have to receive a minimum of 84 correct points for an 80% or passing grade. If your student has received 93 points, simply divide the 93 by 105 for a percentage grade of 89%. Students who receive a score below 80% should review the LIFEPAC and retest using the appropriate Alternate Test found in the Teacher's Guide.

The following is a guideline to assign letter grades for completed LIFEPACs based on a maximum total score of 100 points.

Example:

LIFEPAC Test	=	60% of the Total Score (or percent grade)
Self Test	=	25% of the Total Score (average percent of self tests)
Reports	=	10% or 10* points per LIFEPAC
Oral Work	=	5% or 5* points per LIFEPAC

*Determined by the teacher's subjective evaluation of the student's daily work.

Example:

LIFEPAC Test Score	=	92%	92 × .60	=	55 points
Self Test Average	=	90%	90 × .25	=	23 points
Reports				=	8 points
Oral Work				=	4 points
TOTAL POINTS				=	90 points

Grade Scale based on point system:

100 – 94	=	A
93 – 86	=	B
85 – 77	=	C
76 – 70	=	D
Below 70	=	F

TEACHER HINTS AND STUDYING TECHNIQUES

LIFEPAC activities are written to check the level of understanding of the preceding text. The student may look back to the text as necessary to complete these activities; however, a student should never attempt to do the activities without reading (studying) the text first. Self tests and LIFEPAC tests are never open book tests.

Language arts activities (skill integration) often appear within other subject curriculum. The purpose is to give the student an opportunity to test their skill mastery outside of the context in which it was presented.

Writing complete answers (paragraphs) to some questions is an integral part of the LIFEPAC curriculum in all subjects. This builds communication and organization skills, increases understanding and retention of ideas, and helps enforce good penmanship. Complete sentences should be encouraged for this type of activity. Obviously, single words or phrases do not meet the intent of the activity, since multiple lines are given for the response.

Review is essential to student success. Time invested in review where review is suggested will be time saved in correcting errors later. Self tests, unlike the section activities, are closed book. This procedure helps to identify weaknesses before they become too great to overcome. Certain objectives from self tests are cumulative and test previous sections; therefore, good preparation for a self test must include all material studied up to that testing point.

The following procedure checklist has been found to be successful in developing good study habits in the LIFEPAC curriculum.

1. Read the introduction and Table of Contents.
2. Read the objectives.
3. Recite and study the entire vocabulary (glossary) list.
4. Study each section as follows:
   a. Read the introduction and study the section objectives.
   b. Read all the text for the entire section, but answer none of the activities.
   c. Return to the beginning of the section and memorize each vocabulary word and definition.
   d. Reread the section, complete the activities, check the answers with the answer key, correct all errors, and have the teacher check.
   e. Read the self test but do not answer the questions.
   f. Go to the beginning of the first section and reread the text and answers to the activities up to the self test you have not yet done.
   g. Answer the questions to the self test without looking back.
   h. Have the self test checked by the teacher.
   i. Correct the self test and have the teacher check the corrections.
   j. Repeat steps a–i for each section.
5. Use the **SQ3R** method to prepare for the LIFEPAC test.
   Scan the whole LIFEPAC.
   Question yourself on the objectives.
   Read the whole LIFEPAC again.
   Recite through an oral examination.
   Review weak areas.
6. Take the LIFEPAC test as a closed book test.
7. LIFEPAC tests are administered and scored under direct teacher supervision. Students who receive scores below 80% should review the LIFEPAC using the **SQ3R** study method and take the Alternate Test located in the Teacher's Guide. The final test grade may be the grade on the Alternate Test or an average of the grades from the original LIFEPAC test and the Alternate Test.

GOAL SETTING AND SCHEDULES

Each school must develop its own schedule, because no single set of procedures will fit every situation. The following is an example of a daily schedule that includes the five LIFE-PAC subjects as well as time slotted for special activities.

Possible Daily Schedule

8:15 – 8:25	Pledges, prayer, songs, devotions, etc.
8:25 – 9:10	Bible
9:10 – 9:55	Language Arts
9:55 – 10:15	Recess (juice break)
10:15 – 11:00	Math
11:00 – 11:45	History & Geography
11:45 – 12:30	Lunch, recess, quiet time
12:30 – 1:15	Science
1:15 –	Drill, remedial work, enrichment*

Enrichment: Computer time, physical education, field trips, fun reading, games and puzzles, family business, hobbies, resource persons, guests, crafts, creative work, electives, music appreciation, projects.

Basically, two factors need to be considered when assigning work to a student in the LIFEPAC curriculum.

The first is time. An average of 45 minutes should be devoted to each subject, each day. Remember, this is only an average. Because of extenuating circumstances, a student may spend only 15 minutes on a subject one day and the next day spend 90 minutes on the same subject.

The second factor is the number of pages to be worked in each subject. A single LIFEPAC is designed to take three to four weeks to complete. Allowing about three to four days for LIFEPAC introduction, review, and tests, the student has approximately 15 days to complete the LIFEPAC pages. Simply take the number of pages in the LIFEPAC, divide it by 15 and you will have the number of pages that must be completed on a daily basis to keep the student on schedule. For example, a LIFEPAC containing 45 pages will require three completed pages per day. Again, this is only an average. While working a 45-page LIFEPAC, the student may complete only one page the first day if the text has a lot of activities or reports, but go on to complete five pages the next day.

Long-range planning requires some organization. Because the traditional school year originates in the early fall of one year and continues to late spring of the following year, a calendar should be devised that covers this period of time. Approximate beginning and completion dates can be noted on the calendar as well as special occasions such as holidays, vacations and birthdays. Since each LIFEPAC takes three to four weeks or 18 days to complete, it should take about 180 school days to finish a set of ten LIFEPACs. Starting at the beginning school date, mark off 18 school days on the calendar and that will become the targeted completion date for the first LIFEPAC. Continue marking the calendar until you have established dates for the remaining nine LIFEPACs making adjustments for previously noted holidays and vacations. If all five subjects are being used, the ten established target dates should be the same for the LIFEPACs in each subject.

TEACHING SUPPLEMENTS

The sample weekly lesson plan and student grading sheet forms are included in this section as teacher support materials and may be duplicated at the convenience of the teacher.

The student grading sheet is provided for those who desire to follow the suggested guidelines for assignment of letter grades as previously discussed. The student's self test scores should be posted as percentage grades. When the LIFEPAC is completed the teacher should average the self test grades, multiply the average by .25 and post the points in the box marked self test points. The LIFEPAC percentage grade should be multiplied by .60 and posted. Next, the teacher should award and post points for written reports and oral work. A report may be any type of written work assigned to the student whether it is a LIFEPAC or additional learning activity. Oral work includes the student's ability to respond orally to questions which may or may not be related to LIFEPAC activities or any type of oral report assigned by the teacher. The points may then be totaled and a final grade entered along with the date that the LIFEPAC was completed.

The Student Record Book, which was specifically designed for use with the Alpha Omega curriculum, provides space to record weekly progress for one student over a nine-week period as well as a place to post self test and LIFEPAC scores. The Student Record Books are available through the current Alpha Omega catalog; however, unlike the enclosed forms these books are not for duplication and should be purchased in sets of four to cover a full academic year.

WEEKLY LESSON PLANNER

Week of:

	Subject	Subject	Subject	Subject
Monday				

	Subject	Subject	Subject	Subject
Tuesday				

	Subject	Subject	Subject	Subject
Wednesday				

	Subject	Subject	Subject	Subject
Thursday				

	Subject	Subject	Subject	Subject
Friday				

WEEKLY LESSON PLANNER

Week of:

	Subject	Subject	Subject	Subject
Monday				
Tuesday				
Wednesday				
Thursday				
Friday				

Student Name _____   Year _____

Bible

LP	Self Test Scores by Sections 1	2	3	4	5	Self Test Points	LIFEPAC Test	Oral Points	Report Points	Final Grade	Date
01											
02											
03											
04											
05											
06											
07											
08											
09											
10											

History & Geography

LP	Self Test Scores by Sections 1	2	3	4	5	Self Test Points	LIFEPAC Test	Oral Points	Report Points	Final Grade	Date
01											
02											
03											
04											
05											
06											
07											
08											
09											
10											

Language Arts

LP	Self Test Scores by Sections 1	2	3	4	5	Self Test Points	LIFEPAC Test	Oral Points	Report Points	Final Grade	Date
01											
02											
03											
04											
05											
06											
07											
08											
09											
10											

Student Name _____   Year _____

Math

LP	Self Test Scores by Sections 1	2	3	4	5	Self Test Points	LIFEPAC Test	Oral Points	Report Points	Final Grade	Date
01											
02											
03											
04											
05											
06											
07											
08											
09											
10											

Science

LP	Self Test Scores by Sections 1	2	3	4	5	Self Test Points	LIFEPAC Test	Oral Points	Report Points	Final Grade	Date
01											
02											
03											
04											
05											
06											
07											
08											
09											
10											

Spelling/Electives

LP	Self Test Scores by Sections 1	2	3	4	5	Self Test Points	LIFEPAC Test	Oral Points	Report Points	Final Grade	Date
01											
02											
03											
04											
05											
06											
07											
08											
09											
10											

INSTRUCTIONS FOR HISTORY & GEOGRAPHY

The LIFEPAC curriculum from grades 2 through 12 is structured so that the daily instructional material is written directly into the LIFEPACs. The student is encouraged to read and follow this instructional material in order to develop independent study habits. The teacher should introduce the LIFEPAC to the student, set a required completion schedule, complete teacher checks, be available for questions regarding both content and procedures, administer and grade tests, and develop additional learning activities as desired. Teachers working with several students may schedule their time so that students are assigned to a quiet work activity when it is necessary to spend instructional time with one particular student.

The Teacher Notes section of the Teacher's Guide lists the required or suggested materials for the LIFEPACs and provides additional learning activities for the students. The materials section refers only to LIFEPAC materials and does not include materials which may be needed for the additional activities. Additional learning activities provide a change from the daily school routine, encourage the student's interest in learning and may be used as a reward for good study habits.

HISTORY & GEOGRAPHY 901

Unit 1: Heritage of the United States

TEACHER NOTES

MATERIALS NEEDED FOR LIFEPAC	
Required	Suggested
None	• encyclopedia • reference books or online sources

ADDITIONAL LEARNING ACTIVITIES

Section 1: Historical and Political Backgrounds

1. Discuss this question: What type of person would you have looked for if you were in Europe recruiting colonists for the New World? (Presume that you had already lived for ten years as a pioneer in the New World.)

2. Discuss the following: Suppose the first settlers had come to the Pacific West Coast of the New World. Do you believe the expansion to the East would have been quite as rapid as it was *from* the East?

3. Discuss the following: How much European influence went into the development of United States government and political parties? Describe the effect of the European experience on the ideas expressed in the Declaration of Independence.

4. Have three students (or groups of three students) assume the roles of (a) a general, (b) a president, and (c) a saintly church leader. Tell the class to reflect back on the history of the United States a year before the signing of the Declaration of Independence. Have each student present an argument whether independence from England at the time was a good idea.

5. Using a celebrity-guest format, let each student represent a colony provide a detailed description of life in the region.

6. Using the growth and accomplishments of America as a framework, let a student write a scenario for the development of the United States that does not include conflict or warfare. For example, the student could bring the American people to the same plateaus without the conflicts.

7. Let a student research the early Democratic-Republican Party to discover the degree of continuity the present-day Democratic Party has maintained.

Section 2: Freedom Backgrounds

1. Ask the following questions: How much effect do you feel the new freedom in America had on the colonists? How different was that life from the life they left behind in Europe?

2. Discuss this question: Does it appear that there was a higher degree of inventiveness in America in comparison with the other nations on earth?

3. Have students look over the list of reformers and their accomplishments. Ask students, do you believe these same people would have been as effective in Europe as they were in the United States?

4. Let a student make a list of freedoms enjoyed from the time of the early colonies.

5. From among all the people listed as Freedom Pioneers, let a student write about the person that they feel, more than any other, shaped this country.

Section 3: Society Backgrounds

1. Discuss the following: If you were living in a Western European country in the early 1900s and were seriously considering emigration, what are some of the reasons you would choose America?

2. Let a student select one ethnic group (Italians, Irish, Slavic) and trace the key stages in their emergence as an integral part of American society.

3. Let a student research the decade of the 1960s to determine the major areas of change. Provide the following for consideration and discussion: Does there seem to be another decade in American history that is equal to the 1960s for the changes it brought?

Administer the LIFEPAC Test

The test is to be administered in one session. Give no help except with directions.
Evaluate the tests and review areas where the students have done poorly.
Review the pages and activities that stress the concepts tested.
If necessary, administer the Alternate LIFEPAC Test.

ANSWER KEYS

SECTION 1

1.1   Examples:
  – They were interested in the opportunity to gain wealth and power.
  – The lure of adventure attracted some.
  – The New World was a source of new resources and territories.
  – It was a haven for political and religious freedom.

1.2   Examples:
  – They had to learn new skills.
  – They had to learn to live without comforts.

1.3   America has fertile soil, an abundant water supply, and a bountiful supply of natural resources.

1.4   religious freedom

1.5   William Penn

1.6   Maryland

1.7   Puritans

1.8   England

1.9   Either order:
  a. to gain independence
  b. to overthrow undesirable rulers
  or acquire territory

1.10 Either order:
  a. taxes on various products
  b. acts such as the ones that forced the housing of the British soldiers

1.11 Example:
  War was necessary for the colonists to gain independence and keep the British from taking advantage of them. The colonists wanted to be free from unwanted laws.

1.12 3
1.13 1
1.14 4
1.15 2
1.16 c
1.17 e
1.18 a
1.19 b
1.20 d
1.21 Jefferson
1.22 Tyler
1.23 Polk
1.24 Seward
1.25 Spanish-American
1.26 Panama Canal

1.27 4
1.28 1
1.29 5
1.30 3
1.31 2
1.32 6

1.33 The United States was recognized as a world power after the Spanish-American War.

1.34 Example:
  People thought it was foolish for Secretary of State Seward to pay Russia $7,200,000 for land the public considered worthless.

1.35 Teacher check

1.36 Any order:
  a. charter
  or commercial colony
  b. proprietary colony
  c. royal colony

1.37 Either order:
  a. Federalist Party
  b. Whig Party

1.38 Either order:
  a. Prohibition Party
  b. Socialist Party

1.39 two
1.40 Boston Massacre
1.41 Continental Congress
1.42 Democratic
1.43 Constitution
1.44 to protest the Intolerable Acts
1.45 to take charge of the war and vote for independence

1.46 Examples:
  – They were more loyal to their own states.
  – They had different forms of government.
  – They had become very independent.
  – Some wanted a "weak" central government.

SELF TEST 1

1.01 e
1.02 c
1.03 f
1.04 a
1.05 d
1.06 g
1.07 b
1.08 heritage
1.09 Either order:
a. Sodom
b. Gomorrah
1.010 Any order:
a. wealth
b. power
c. adventure
1.011 Examples:
Hitler
or Castro
1.012 a. taxes
b. acts
1.013 Any order:
a. commercial charter
or commercial
b. royal
c. proprietary
1.014 Either order:
a. Federalists
b. Democratic-Republicans
1.015 Puritans
1.016 false
1.017 true
1.018 false
1.019 true
1.020 true
1.021 false
1.022 c
1.023 a
1.024 b
1.025 c
1.026 a

SECTION 2

2.1 Religious freedom is the right to worship God as one sees fit without interference from anyone or any government.
2.2 Our religious freedom is guaranteed by the First Amendment to the United States Constitution.
2.3 We should use our freedoms to the extent that we do not impose on other people's freedoms.
2.4 Examples; any order:
a. Freedom of religion
b. Freedom of speech
c. Freedom of the press
d. Right to assemble peacefully
e. Right to petition the government
2.5 Examples; any order:
a. cotton gin
b. steam engine
c. airplane
d. automobile
e. polio vaccine
2.6 Examples; any order:
a. lawmakers
b. inventors
c. religious leaders
d. scientists
e. professionals
or authors, educators, reformers, artists, entertainers, or statesmen
2.7 steam engine
2.8 storms
2.9 polio
2.10 Wright brothers
2.11 A system of mass production
2.12 Example:
They had given us laws which protect our freedoms.
2.13 Example:
They have given us things which make our lives easier and increase our production.
2.14 Example:
They have increased our life spans and taken away our fear of certain diseases.

SELF TEST 2

2.01 Either order:
   a. freedom
   b. equality
2.02 religious freedom
2.03 religious leaders
2.04 Example:
   Mark Twain
2.05 Philadelphia
2.06 Examples; any order:
   a. cotton gin
   b. steam engine
   c. automobile
2.07 true
2.08 false
2.09 false
2.010 true
2.011 false
2.012 e
2.013 b
2.014 d
2.015 f
2.016 a
2.017 c
2.018 a
2.019 b
2.020 b
2.021 c
2.022 They worked in the home, raised children, and managed the household.
2.023 The first amendment to the Constitution grants us this freedom.

SECTION 3

3.1 true
3.2 false
3.3 false
3.4 true
3.5 true
3.6 People of many backgrounds have fit so well into the American society that they appear as everyone else.
3.7 Examples; any order:
   a. To escape natural catastrophes
   b. To escape war
   c. To escape tyranny or to find freedom
   d. To seek higher standard of living
   e. Because they are forced to leave
3.8 family
3.9 Depression
3.10 mobility
3.11 God
   or Christianity
3.12 God
3.13 – It has changed our homes, our thoughts, our beliefs, our entire way of life.
   – It introduced the machine age and fostered technology and invention.
3.14 A return to the Christian principles stressed in the Bible may save American family life.
3.15 Teacher check

SELF TEST 3

3.01 c
3.02 e
3.03 b
3.04 a
3.05 d
3.06 true
3.07 true
3.08 false
3.09 true
3.010 true
3.011 d
3.012 d
3.013 a
3.014 c
3.015 a
3.016 family
3.017 change
3.018 mobility
3.019 Any order:
  a. instant
  b. junk-food
  c. fast-food
3.020 Quakers
3.021 Jefferson
3.022 First Amendment
3.023 steam engine
3.024 The U.S. became recognized as a world power.
3.025 Washington refused to run for a third term, thus setting a precedent of a two-term limit for presidents.
3.026 He initiated a system of mass production.
3.027 Although public schools began in the United States to teach children to read the Bible, the Supreme Court has ruled that Bible reading in the public schools is unconstitutional.

LIFEPAC TEST

1. false
2. true
3. true
4. false
5. false
6. false
7. false
8. false
9. false
10. true
11. c
12. e
13. f
14. d
15. a
16. b
17. c
18. a
19. c
20. b
21. Any order:
   a. charter
   or commercial
   b. proprietary
   c. royal colony
22. Either order:
   a. gain independence
   b. overthrow undesirable rulers
   or acquire territory
23. Any order:
   a. lawmakers
   b. religious leaders
   c. inventors
   or scientists, professionals, authors,
       educators, reformers, artists, entertainers
24. family
25. Declaration of Independence
26. A return to the Christian principles stressed
    in the Bible may save family life.
27. People of many backgrounds have fit so well
    into the American society that they appear as
    everyone else.

ALTERNATE LIFEPAC TEST

1. false
2. false
3. true
4. false
5. false
6. true
7. false
8. false
9. false
10. true
11. f
12. e
13. a
14. b
15. c
16. d
17. a
18. c
19. b
20. b
21. Democratic
22. George Washington
23. Florence Nightingale
24. family
25. changes
26. Example:
    Because the proprietary colonies were
    being governed in so many ways:
    Charter, Proprietary, Royal Colony.
27. Example:
    It has affected industry, but it has also
    revolutionized our homes, our thoughts,
    our beliefs, and our entire way of life.

HISTORY & GEOGRAPHY 901

ALTERNATE LIFEPAC TEST

NAME _____

DATE _____

SCORE _____

59
74

Answer *true* or *false* (each answer, 2 points).

1. _____ President John Tyler was the first president to purchase land for the United States.

2. _____ The United States acquired the Panama Canal as the result of the Spanish-American War.

3. _____ The French and Indian War preceded the War of 1812.

4. _____ The writers of the Declaration of Independence avoided letting the Bible influence what they authored.

5. _____ Horace Mann has been called the "Father of the American novel."

6. _____ Most of the early colonists came to America to escape the tyranny which existed under the rule of kings.

7. _____ The idea of freedom without responsibility was the rule in America from its birth.

8. _____ Europe has been termed the "melting pot of the world."

9. _____ Most people living in a controlled society appreciate the security that control brings, and they fear freedom.

10. _____ Mobility has brought about a severe weakening of the family in the United States today.

Match these items (each answer, 2 points).

11. _____ Maryland   a. responsible for the Louisiana Purchase

12. _____ Jonas Salk   b. the potato famine

13. _____ Thomas Jefferson   c. colony for Quakers

14. _____ Ireland   d. made the first airplane flight

15. _____ Pennsylvania   e. discovered a polio vaccine

16. _____ Wright brothers   f. colony for Catholics

                                          g. purchased Alaska

Write the letter for the correct answer on each line (each answer, 3 points).

17. The settlers who got along best with the Native Americans were the _____ .
    a. French   b. British   c. Italians   d. Spanish

18. Florida was obtained from the _____ .
    a. French   b. British   c. Spanish   d. Portuguese

19. The invention that led to the development of better water transportation and the railroad
    was the _____ .
    a. wheel   b. steam engine   c. gasoline engine   d. steel casting

20. The only group of immigrants that has not lost its identity is the _____ .
    a. Germans   b. Jews   c. French   d. Irish

Complete these statements (each answer, 4 points).

21. The Democratic-Republican Party later became the _____ Party.

22. The first American president to serve two terms was _____

    _____ .

23. Sanitary methods for caring for the sick and wounded, which lessened the number of cases

    of typhus, cholera, and dysentery, were introduced by a nurse named _____

    _____ .

24. One of the most important ingredients in the success of this country has been the social unit

    called the _____ .

25. Since 1963 our society has made many _____ .

Answer these questions (each answer, 5 points).

26. Why did the colonies have difficulty uniting?

_____

_____

_____

_____

27. What effect has the Industrial Revolution had on our society?

_____

_____

_____

_____

HISTORY & GEOGRAPHY 902

Unit 2: Our National Government

TEACHER NOTES

MATERIALS NEEDED FOR LIFEPAC	
Required	Suggested
None	• copy of the Declaration of Independence • encyclopedia • reference books or online sources

ADDITIONAL LEARNING ACTIVITIES

Section 1: The Ideals of Our National Government

1. Discuss the following questions: How does our national government protect the rights of citizens? Does the national government intrude on our rights in any way? How? What can be done about it?

2. Discuss the following questions: How old does a United States citizen have to be to vote? Do you intend to vote when you reach that age? Is it important? Why, or why not?

3. Tell partners to discuss Jefferson's statement that "...all men are created equal" in order define what he means and apply the phrase.

4. Have students select one of the Founding Fathers of our country such as Thomas Jefferson or Benjamin Franklin, and write a short biography of his life and achievements. Students should discuss what they think the person's most outstanding accomplishment or accomplishments were.

5. Tell students to list the ways God has blessed our country. Discuss: Are you grateful for these blessings? How can you show your gratitude?

Section 2: Development of Our National Government

1. Guide students to think of a country which recently had a revolution and overthrew its government. Discuss: Is the new government in that country a success? How did the recent revolution compare with our own American Revolution and its outcome?

2. The Constitution of the United States has only been amended twenty-seven times in 250 years. Together, name one or two proposed amendments that have drawn national attention in recent years. Ask students if they support these amendments (explain).

3. As a class, make two charts, one showing the major features of the Articles of Confederation, the other showing the features of the Constitution. Discuss why the articles had to be discarded and how the Constitution remedied their defects.

4. Have students write a paragraph on the meaning of the word *federal* and how it applies to our national government today. The paragraph should address the following: Which is more powerful, the national or the state government?

Section 3: The Legislative Branch — Congress

1. Ask these questions: What does *bicameral* mean? How does it apply to Congress? Explain.

2. Tell students to think of a law they would like to see passed and describe the process it would have to go through to be passed by Congress.

3. Tell students to pretend that they are running for the United States Congress. Have them make a speech that states their qualifications and the most important national problems they would like to help solve.

4. Instruct students to find a recent news or magazine story about a new law that has been passed by Congress. Have the class or partners discuss: Does it seem to you to be a good law? Why, or why not?

5. Have students find out the boundaries of your own congressional district, and describe them in a brief report, answering these questions: How many people are in your district? Who is your congressperson?

Section 4: The Executive Branch — The President

1. Discuss the following: How is the president elected? Why did the framers of the Constitution decide on the electoral college? Is it still necessary? Is it still a good idea?

2. Ask these questions: Would you like to be elected president of the United States someday? How much money would you make? What qualifications would you have to meet?

3. Conduct a mock Cabinet meeting. According to the number of students available, let there be a president and important Cabinet heads. Have each Cabinet member deliver a brief report on the state of his or her department.

4. Ask these questions: How many presidential administrations have you lived under? How many presidents have your parents lived under? Ask them who their favorite president was, and why they feel that way.

5. Have the class use recent news magazines, newspapers, and news reports to make a list of at least three positions the president of the United States has taken on recent issues. Ask students, do you think these positions will make him more, or less, popular with the Congress and the American people?

Section 5: The Judicial Branch

1. Assign students to write a 250-word report on the makeup of the United States Supreme Court and what it does. They can use an encyclopedia, other reference work, or online resources in addition to the information presented in the LIFEPAC.

2. Assign students to write a brief biography of a well-known justice of the Supreme Court such as John Marshall, Oliver Wendell Holmes or Thurgood Marshall. Instruct them to include his major accomplishments and the things for which he is best remembered.

3. Have students use an almanac or online sources to list the current justices of the United States Supreme Court. Ask, who is the Chief Justice? Students should locate a picture of the justices and label the justices' names.

Administer the LIFEPAC Test

ANSWER KEYS

SECTION 1

1.1	those who are governed by it
1.2	our God-given rights
1.3	forming our present government
1.4	Any order:
	a. to form a more perfect union
	b. to establish justice
	c. to insure domestic tranquility
	d. to provide for the common defense
	e. to promote the general welfare
	f. to secure blessings of liberty to ourselves and our posterity
1.5	a government in which all the people meet together and are directly involved in making laws and deciding on government action
1.6	a democracy in which the people elect others to speak for them
1.7	a type of representative democracy in which the representatives are limited by the Constitution and the people's individual rights are protected
1.8	the people of the United States give our government its authority and, therefore, the people are the government
1.9	a. federal
	b. state
1.10	a. IV
	b. republican
1.11	a representative government
1.12	federal
1.13	any leader of small group from trying to take over all the power of the government
1.14	Each branch of government has power to check the powers of the other two branches.
1.15	Any order:
	a. legislative
	b. executive
	c. judicial
1.16	The system of checks and balances prevents any one branch of government from getting too powerful and dominating the other branches.

SELF TEST 1

1.01	c
1.02	f
1.03	a
1.04	i
1.05	j
1.06	e
1.07	b
1.08	g
1.09	d
1.010	h
1.011	k
1.012	l
1.013	Any order:
	a. to form a more perfect union
	b. to establish justice
	c. to insure domestic tranquility
	d. to provide for the common defense
	e. to promote the general welfare
	f. to secure the blessings of liberty to ourselves and our posterity
1.014	to protect the rights of its citizens
1.015	the citizens
1.016	democracy
1.017	Any order:
	a. government by the consent of the governed
	b. government by representation
	c. government with limited powers and separate powers
	d. system of checks and balances (federal system of government)
1.018	a. enforces the laws
	b. makes the laws
	c. interprets the laws
1.019	a. presidential veto of a passed bill
	b. override a presidential veto with two-thirds vote of each house
	c. declare a law unconstitutional

SECTION 2

2.1 Parliament

2.2 Mayflower Compact

2.3 the first written plan of government

2.4 the king and Parliament

2.5 First Continental Congress

2.6 Any order:

    a. provided the government during the Revolutionary War

    b. wrote and adopted the Declaration of Independence

    c. wrote the Articles of Confederation

2.7 Teacher check

2.8 the necessities of war gave its decisions popular support

2.9 "firm league of friendship"

2.10 west of the Appalachian Mountains

2.11 They feared creating too strong a government that would take away their liberties or interfere in local affairs.

2.12 a. Confederation Congress

    b. advisory

2.13 Any order:

    a. Nine votes of Congress were needed to pass laws and all thirteen votes were needed to pass amendments.

    b. The Continental Congress had no power to tax and no court system.

    c. The Congress had no power to raise armies and could not enforce treaties.

2.14 Shay's

2.15 having enough members present to make the work legal

2.16 to revise the Articles of Confederation.

2.17 Teacher check

2.18 to revise the Articles of Confederation

2.19 b. plural executive

2.20 A two-house legislature:

    – lower house representation according to population

    – upper house by equal representation

2.21 Include following information:

    – The members of the electoral college represent the general population in presidential elections.

    – Each state has electors equal in number to the state's number of representatives and senators in Congress.

    – The electors of a state generally vote the same way as does the general population.

2.22 nine

2.23 Anti-Federalist

2.24 Federalist

2.25 1788

2.26 Preamble

2.27 seven

2.28 Article I created legislative branch, with structure, duties, and powers of Congress.

Article II created executive branch, with enforcement of laws by president and aides.

Article III created judicial branch, with Supreme Court and federal court system.

Article IV states relationship with federal and other state governments.

Article V tells ways of proposing amendments and ratifying them.

Article VI gives general provisions.

Article VII states ratification procedure.

2.29 An amendment changes or adds to the Constitution.

2.30 twenty-seven

2.31 a. Bill of Rights

    b. individual liberties

2.32 Teacher check

SELF TEST 2

2.01   f
2.02   c
2.03   m
2.04   a
2.05   n
2.06   j
2.07   d
2.08   b
2.09   h
2.010 g
2.011 o
2.012 l
2.013 e
2.014 i
2.015 three-fifths of the slaves would be counted for both taxation and population purposes
2.016 federal
2.017 the Second Continental Congress
2.018 the writers feared a strong central government that might take away their liberties or interfere in local affairs
2.019 to revise the Articles of Confederation
2.020 two
2.021 to protect individual liberties
2.022 the King was violating the colonists' individual liberties
2.023 b
2.024 a
2.025 b
2.026 a
2.027 c
2.028 a. created legislative branch, with structure, duties, and powers of Congress
       b. created executive branch, with enforcement of laws by president and aides
       c. created judicial branch, with Supreme Court and federal court system
       d. states relationship with federal and other state governments
       e. tells way of proposing amendments and ratifying them
       f. gives general provisions
       g. state's ratification process

2.029 Any order; any six:
       a. freedom of speech
       b. freedom of press
       c. freedom of religion
       d. right to assembly
       e. right to petition
       f. trial by jury
       or cannot be compelled to speak against oneself, speedy and public trial, right to bear arms, cannot be compelled to quarter troops, secure against unreasonable search and seizure, excessive bail

SECTION 3

3.1   a. Congress
Either order:
b. Senate
c. House of Representatives

3.2   Either order:
a. to settle disputes in the Constitutional Convention
b. to provide a system of checks and balances within Congress

3.3   a. 435
b. 2

3.4   c. two-year

3.5   counting of the country's population

3.6   Any order:
a. must be at least twenty-five years old
b. must be a citizen for at least seven years
c. must live in the state in which they are elected

3.7   a representative who is elected by all state voters, not just one district.

3.8   seventeenth amendment

3.9 $174,000

3.10   being forced to resign from office after two-thirds of both houses vote in favor of this action.

3.11   Any order:
a. Parliamentarian; answers questions concerning parliamentary procedure.
b. Sergeant at Arms; prevents trouble from occurring on the Congress floor.
c. pages; run errands and provide needed materials

3.12   January 3rd

3.13   Teacher check

3.14   a. the floor leader from the majority party
b. the floor leader from the minority party
c. party meetings to determine party policies and actions
d. assist party whip to guide laws party wants through Congress; decides what bills to support
e. permanent committees

3.15   a. vice president
b. Speaker of the House

3.16   President Pro-Tempore

3.17   committees

3.18   nominations from committee on committees and member from each house choosing from nominees

3.19   Example:
The chair person would be able to determine what bills the committee would consider, allowing them to push their party bills more easily.

3.20   Any order:
a. expressed
b. implied
c. inherent

3.21   Any order:
a. financing the government
b. regulating and encouraging trade and industry
c. defending our nation against its enemies
d. enforcing nation's laws
e. providing for the growth of our nation

3.22   elastic

3.23   Any order:
a. public opinion
b. Constitution
c. Supreme Court

3.24   Either order:
a. approves treaties and appointments
b. override the veto by two-thirds vote in both houses

3.25   Teacher check

3.26   Across
1. expulsion
2. chairman
4. whip
7. steering
8. bicameral
12. governed
13. caucus
14. pigeonholed
Down
1. elastic
3. executive
5. page
6. speaker
9. large
10. January
11. committee

3.27   a.   8
        b.   11
        c.   1
        d.   17
        e.   5
        f.   2
        g.   4
        h.   19
        i.   13
        j.   7
        k.   3
        l.   15
        m. 20
        n.   9
        o.   12
        p.   18
        q.   16
        r.   14
        s.   10
        t.   6
3.28   Teacher check
3.29   Teacher check

SELF TEST 3

3.01   true
3.02   true
3.03   false
3.04   true
3.05   false
3.06   false
3.07   true
3.08   true
3.09   false
3.010 false
3.011 true
3.012 f
3.013 c
3.014 k
3.015 i
3.016 a
3.017 j
3.018 e
3.019 h
3.020 g
3.021 b
3.022 Any order:
      a.   executive
      b.   legislative
      c.   judicial
3.023 Either order:
      a.   House of Representatives
      b.   Senate
3.024 a.   vice president
      b.   President Pro-Tempore
3.025 Any order:
      a.   Supreme Court
      b.   Constitution
      c.   public opinion
3.026 Any order:
      a.   expressed
      b.   implied
      c.   inherent
3.027 president
3.028 Any order:
      a.   A representative must be at least twenty-five years old
      b.   must have been a citizen for at least seven years
      c.   must live in the state in which they were elected

3.029 Any order:
  a. must be at least thirty years old
  b. must be a citizen for nine years
  c. must live in the state in which they are elected
3.030 a. The bill is introduced into the House of Representatives.
  b. The bill is sent to a House committee.
  c. The bill is returned to the house.
  d. The House votes on the bill.
  e. The Senate receives the bill.
  f. The bill is sent to the Senate committee.
  g. The bill is sent to the Senate.
  h. The bill goes to the president.

SECTION 4

4.1 Any order:
  a. must be at least thirty-five years old
  b. must be a native-born citizen
  c. must be a resident of the United States for fourteen years
4.2 a. 4
  b. 10
4.3 electoral college
4.4 Since all the electoral votes of a state go to one candidate, it is possible that by losing by a close popular vote in enough large states the one candidate could receive more voters than the other candidate but lose by not gaining enough electors.
4.5 $400,000 a year
4.6 Chief Executive
4.7 Any order:
  a. the State of the Union Address
  b. the Economic Message
  c. the Budget Message
4.8 veto
4.9 Commander-in-Chief planning the strategy
4.10 foreign
4.11 a. cabinet
  b. ambassadors
  c. Supreme Court
4.12 Any order:
  a. pardons
  b. reprieves
  c. commutation
4.13 the Senate
4.14 State Department
4.15 Department of Defense
4.16 Department of Interior
4.17 Department of Transportation
4.18 Department of Energy
4.19 Department of Commerce
4.20 Department of the Treasury
4.21 Department of the Treasury
4.22 Department of the Agriculture
4.23 Department of Labor
4.24 Department of Housing and Urban Development
4.25 Department of Education
4.26 Department of Health and Human Services
4.27 Department of Justice
4.28 State Department

4.29   Department of Defense
4.30   Department of Homeland Security
4.31   Department of Health and Human Services
4.32   Department of Agriculture
4.33   Department of Commerce
4.34   Department of Commerce
4.35   Cabinet
4.36   a.   fifteen
       b.   Executive Department
4.37   Any order:
       a.   ambassadors
       b.   ministers
       c.   consuls
4.38   Either order:
       a.   White House Staff
       b.   Executive Office

SELF TEST 4

4.01   Cabinet
4.02   Either order:
       a.   Senate
       b.   House of Representatives
4.03   enforcing
4.04   electoral college
4.05   January 3rd
4.06   Inauguration
4.07   a.   House of Representatives
       b.   Senate
4.08   Chief
4.09   State of the Union
4.010   P
4.011   C
4.012   C
4.013   P
4.014   P
4.015   C
4.016   P
4.017   C
4.018   P
4.019   P
4.020   Department of Commerce
4.021   Department of Justice
4.022   Department of Energy
4.023   Department of Homeland Security
4.024   Department of Treasury
4.025   Department of Health and Human Services
4.026   Any order:
       a.   must be at least thirty-five years old
       b.   must be a native-born citizen
       c.   must be a resident of the United States for fourteen years
4.027   Any order:
       a.   must be at least thirty-years old
       b.   must be a citizen of the United States for at least nine years
       c.   must be a legal resident of the state represented
4.028   Any order:
       a.   must be at least twenty-five years old
       b.   must be a citizen of the United States for at least seven years
       c.   must be a legal resident of the state represented
4.029   e
4.030   h
4.031   a
4.032   g
4.033   d
4.034   b
4.035   f

SECTION 5

5.1 the Supreme Court and inferior courts
5.2 Congress
5.3 Judiciary Act of 1789
5.4 Any order:
    a. Supreme Court
    b. District Courts
5.5 something that is just and reasonable or right
5.6 the Judicial Code
5.7 District Court
5.8 federal crimes and civil suits arising from postal, patent, copyright, Internal Revenue, and bankruptcy laws
5.9 Any order:
    a. U.S. Marshal
    b. Federal Commissioner
    c. U.S. District Attorney
5.10 appealed
5.11 a. Three
    b. whether the person who appealed the case was granted his full legal rights
5.12 a. about ninety
    b. eleven
5.13 the Supreme Court
5.14 a. nine
    b. president
    c. life
5.15 Judicial Review
5.16 a. consuls, ambassadors, ministers to foreign nations
    b. state
5.17 Supreme Court
5.18 a written order to call a case up from a lower court for review
5.19 a. Court
    b. Amendment
5.20 d
5.21 a
5.22 e
5.23 c

SELF TEST 5

5.01 Judicial Code
5.02 Courts of the United States
5.03 District
5.04 Supreme Court
5.05 three
5.06 Judicial Review
5.07 Nine
5.08 The Supreme Court
5.09 Supreme Court
5.010 Customs Court
5.011 Court of Claims
5.012 Tax Court
5.013 b
5.014 c
5.015 b
5.016 c
5.017 c
5.018 c
5.019 c
5.020 b
5.021 federal crimes and civil suits arising from postal, patent, copyright, internal revenue, and bankruptcy laws
5.022 ambassadors, consuls, ministers to foreign countries, and cases involving state governments
5.023 a written order to call a case up from a lower court for review
5.024 whether the person who appealed the case was granted his full legal rights
5.025 a. created legislative branch, with structure duties, and powers of Congress
    b. created executive branch, with enforcement of laws by president and aides
    c. created judicial branch with Supreme Court and federal court system
    d. states relationship with federal and other state governments
    e. tells way of proposing amendments and ratifying them
    f. gives general provisions
    g. states ratification process

LIFEPAC TEST

1. true
2. true
3. false
4. true
5. false
6. true
7. rights
8. democracy
9. Any order:
   a. legislature
   b. executive
   c. judicial
10. Second Continental Congress
11. Either order:
    a. Senate
    b. House or Representatives
12. Large
13. President Pro-Tempore
14. Commander-in-Chief
15. veto
16. district court
17. Supreme Court
18. b
19. b *or* c
20. b
21. c
22. c
23. c
24. b
25. a
26. d
27. d
28. g
29. j
30. a
31. c
32. e
33. i
34. m
35. h
36. k
37. l
38. d
39. b
40. n

ALTERNATE LIFEPAC TEST

1. false
2. true
3. false
4. true
5. true
6. true
7. true
8. revise the articles
9. federal
10. democracy
11. vice president
12. Any order:
    a. executive
    b. legislative
    c. judicial
13. advisory
14. veto
15. large
16. rights
17. Second Continental Congress
18. Chief
19. d
20. b
21. d
22. b
23. a
24. a
25. c
26. b
27. c
28. d
29. k
30. g
31. m
32. l
33. i
34. f
35. c
36. b
37. j
38. a
39. h
40. e

HISTORY & GEOGRAPHY 902

ALTERNATE LIFEPAC TEST

NAME _____

DATE _____

SCORE _____

72

90

Answer *true* **or** *false* (each answer, 1 point).

1. _____ All bills start in the House of Representatives except for money bills.

2. _____ The elastic clause states that the Congress can pass all laws necessary and proper to carry out its duties.

3. _____ The president has the power to declare war.

4. _____ Placing aside a bill in committee is called pigeonholing.

5. _____ The Supreme Court has original jurisdiction in cases involving United States ambassadors.

6. _____ There are three judges who sit on the court of appeals to hear cases.

7. _____ Congress can override a veto by a two-thirds vote in both houses.

Complete these statements (each answer, 3 points).

8. The purpose for the Constitutional Convention was to _____ .

9. In a federal system of government the _____ government is stronger than all other governments.

10. A government where the people control their own affairs is called a(n) _____ .

11. The presiding officer of the Senate is the _____ .

12. The three branches which make up the government are a. _____ ,

   b. _____ , and c. _____ .

13. The Articles of Confederation provided for the Confederation Congress, but it was little more than a(n) _____ council.

14. The president has the power to _____ bills that they oppose.

15. A representative who is elected by all of the voters of the state is called a congressman-at-_____ .

16. The purpose of our national government is to protect the _____ of its citizens.

17. The government that governed the United States during the Revolutionary War was the

    _____ .

18. Since the president leads the executive branch of government, they are sometimes referred to as the _____ Executive.

Write the letter for the correct answer on each line (each answer, 2 points).

19. The powers of Congress are limited by _____ .
    a. The Constitution   b. The Supreme Court   c. public opinion   d. all of these

20. All of the following items are types of powers that the Congress has *except* _____ powers.
    a. inherent   b. ad hoc   c. implied   d. expressed

21. The committee that helps the party whip guide laws through Congress is the _____ committee.
    a. standing   b. ad hoc   c. special   d. steering

22. The congressional aide who runs errands for congressmen is the _____ .
    a. parliamentarian   b. page   c. chief of staff   d. sergeant at arms

23. The Senate has _____ members.
    a. 100   b. 345   c. 435   d. 534

24. A representative serves _____ -year terms.
    a. two   b. four   c. six   d. unlimited

25. All of the following items were weaknesses of the Articles of Confederation *except* _____ .
    a. inability to call troops   b. inability to tax
    c. inability to make treaties   d. no courts to settle disputes

26. All of the following are parts of the Constitution *except* _____ .
    a. amendments   b. resolution for independence
    c. seven articles   d. Preamble

27.   The United States has a _____ democracy.
      a. direct   b. representative   c. constitutional   d. socialistic

28.   The government receives its authority from the consent of the _____ .
      a. Congress   b. president   c. Supreme Court   d. governed

Match these items (each answer, 2 points).

29.   _____   James Madison   a. method of electing presidents

30.   _____   Shay's Rebellion   b. makes the laws

31.   _____   speaker   c. limits government power

32.   _____   cabinet   d. forced to resign

33.   _____   inauguration   e. provided for a weak government

34.   _____   writ of certiorari   f. appeal to higher authority

35.   _____   checks and balances   g. showed need for a stronger government

36.   _____   legislative   h. decide if a law is constitutional

37.   _____   census   i. president's swearing-in ceremony

38.   _____   electoral college   j. counting the population

39.   _____   judicial review   k. "father of the Constitution"

40.   _____   Articles of Confederation   l. president's chief advisors

                                               m. presiding officer of the House

HISTORY & GEOGRAPHY 903

Unit 3: State and Local Government

TEACHER NOTES

MATERIALS NEEDED FOR LIFEPAC	
Required	Suggested
None	• dictionary of American History • *Encyclopedia Americana* • reference books or online sources

ADDITIONAL LEARNING ACTIVITIES

Section 1: State Government in a Democracy

1. Discuss the following: Do you feel your state government is serving and protecting you? If so, name a few specific areas where, without that service, you would suffer loss or deprivation.

2. Ask these questions: What is the relationship between your state and your school? What degree of control do you suppose the state exercises over your school?

3. Guide students through the following questions: Could you describe the pattern of the national Constitution as it provides the basis for state constitutions? Examine the "shared powers" portion of the diagram: does this describe the pattern? Teacher: See Article 4, Section 4 of the United States Constitution.

4. Ask students to name the three main divisions of state government and break each of them down into some of its basic parts.

5. Ask students how they would respond to the person who states, "My vote does not count!"?

6. As a class, discuss the responsibilities of citizens in the United States.

7. In order to bring out the responsibilities of the states to its citizens, let each student take one of those responsibilities (e.g., elections, education, laws concerning marriage, etc.) and represent their area as being the most important, explaining their points.

8. Divide the class into two groups; federalists and localists.
   Let the students debate the issue: *more power to the federal government vs. more power to the state government*.

9. In an effort to better grasp the function of each of the three divisions of government, set up a mock issue which would alternately affect all three. Divide the class into three groups. Sample issue: introduction of a tougher anti-abortion law.

10. Have the class make a poster using the Governments of States chart. Over the next week let students bring news clippings or print outs regarding the three key offices or officers. Tack the clippings to the appropriate place on the poster.

11. Divide the class into two groups. Let one side argue the issue: *rights without responsibility*. Let the other side argue the point: *rights with responsibility*.

12. Plan to attend an open board of education meeting as a group. The purpose for students is to discern the types of matters for which this group is responsible.

13. Have the student draw up an itemized list of services the state performs for each family member.

14. Instruct the students to determine the cost per family member for services supplied by the state. This can be determined by the amount of state taxes that parents paid, along with an estimate of sales, gas, and other taxes.

15. Let a student research the state constitution to determine (a) the major areas of variance with the federal Constitution and (b) the areas of distinct advantages of his state constitution over other *standard* constitutions.

16. Let a student research the history of the state's original constitution: the persons who influenced it, the problems that developed with it, and the degree of variance with the present constitution.

17. Assign students to write a report on instances where only a few votes decided a major election (for governor, mayor, senator, or within the Electoral College for a president).

18. Arrange for students to meet with a local government representative to ask about their views on the importance of the individual citizen in the governmental process.

Section 2: County and Township Governments

1. Discuss the following: Could you conceive of a township operating independently of its state? What do you imagine the advantage or disadvantage of such a policy would be?

2. Ask these questions: How did counties and townships develop historically? What control over the establishment of townships does the state have?

3. Ask students if they know any of your county or township officials? How much time (average) do you suppose they devote to their governmental duties weekly, monthly, and annually?

4. Ask students if they could you name a half-dozen county officials and offer a thumbnail sketch of their duties.

5. Ask students, how much variation is there in the form of government of the nation's 3,000 counties?

6. Discuss the following: What do you think of the county manager concept? Do you know enough about the workings of your present county government to be able to say whether the county manager type of government would be more efficient?

7. Divide the class into three groups (representing township, county, and state government officials), and instruct each group to find issues that would be addressed in their agency. Then, have the class find several issues that would have to go through all three agencies.

8. Present the following scenario: Let's cut taxes by eliminating town and county government and increasing the work load and personnel of the state government.

9. Plan to attend a meeting of the local town council.

10. Plan to attend a meeting of the county board of supervisors.

11. Having students debate the following issue after having time to research: *"Resolved: we should adopt a county manager type of government."*

12. Help students obtain a copy of your town charter and constitution, and assign them to write a report on how the town is specifically related to the state government.

13. Help students obtain a copy of your county's constitution and have them determine how it is directly responsible to the state.

14. Arrange a visit to the local party headquarters of your town's mayor or county supervisor, and have students pick up some publicity or campaign literature regarding the mayor's or supervisor's performance and goals.

15. After students have determined the specific duties of a particular county or town official, instruct them to draw up their own county manager plan of how to best serve the citizens and address issues.

16. Assign students to write a letter to the editor of your local newspaper, advocating adoption of the county manager plan.

Section 3: City Government

1. Discuss the following: How are village and city governments alike and dissimilar? What is the difference between a commission and a department?

2. Ask students to describe the relationship between the city government and the state legislature.

3. Ask, which type of government does your city have?

4. After reviewing the types of city government, ask students which they feel is the strongest and most efficient.

5. Ask these questions: Are you aware of changes in your city? Do you feel the effort and expense of renovating the city can be justified?

6. Discuss how the news portrays crime in your city. Does it give the impression that it is widespread?

7. Plan to attend a meeting of the city council.

8. As a class, debate the issue of a weak versus a strong mayor plan.

9. Let each student present a case for the (a) mayor-council plan, (b) commission plan, and (c) city manager plan. Then vote for one of the three on the basis of the arguments presented.

10. Have the class gather news and information about criticism of the present city government in order to determine the presence or absence of Biblical truth in these arguments.

11. Assign a group of students to gather information on a recent or planned urban renewal program in your area.

12. Have students write a report on three city governments in the present decade, emphasizing how their success or failure to meet the needs of their citizens reflects on the type of city government they have employed.

13. Assign students to write a research paper on the charter of the city in which they live, with emphasis on how the charter affects their family in daily living.

14. Have students use the local library or newspaper website to review the editorials of the city newspaper over the past few months as they criticize or praise the city government. Instruct students to analyze whether the praise or criticism seems to be justified in light of the complexity of issues dealt with by the city government.

15. Have students research a type of city government not in use in your city, and then write a letter to the editor of your city paper advocating the plan they have researched.

16. Acquire a set of pictures of the nearest city before and after the most recent urban-renewal program. You may have to obtain back issues of the city paper or the city hall may be able to supply them. You can also try checking the website for the city. Present and discuss in class.

Administer the LIFEPAC Test

The test is to be administered in one session. Give no help except with directions.
Evaluate the tests and review areas where the students have done poorly.
Review the pages and activities that stress the concepts tested.
If necessary, administer the Alternate LIFEPAC Test.

ANSWER KEYS

SECTION 1

1.1 a. people
      b. territory
      c. government
      d. controls
1.2 Articles of Confederation
1.3 Any order:
      a. regulate trade between the states
      b. conduct foreign affairs
      c. print and coin money
      d. set up a postal service
      e. build an army and navy
1.4 states
1.5 Any order:
      a. elections
      b. voting qualifications
      c. education
      d. marriage and divorce
      e. traffic laws
      or speed limits and highway safety;
          establish city, town, township, and county
          governments
1.6 concurrent powers
1.7 taxation
1.8 Any order
      a. gasoline
      b. alcoholic beverage
      c. cigarettes
      d. real estate
      e. income
      or personal property
1.9 Either order:
      a. for emergencies such as floods,
          tornadoes, other natural disasters to
          communities
      b. for use during war time
      or to help preserve law and order
1.10 true
1.11 false
1.12 true
1.13 false
1.14 true
1.15 true
1.16 false
1.17 true
1.18 false
1.19 true

1.20 Any order:
      a. draw up state budgets
      b. propose taxes
      c. overseas spending of public funds
      d. call out national guard
1.21 Any order:
      a. executive
      b. legislative
      c. judicial
1.22 a. Senate
      b. House of Representatives or general
          assembly
      c. Nebraska
1.23 a. 21
      b. 25
1.24 a. New Hampshire
      b. California
1.25 a. four-year
      b. two-year
1.26 Any order:
      a. Alabama
      b. Louisiana
      c. Maryland
      d. Mississippi
1.27 Senate
1.28 Speaker of the House
1.29 Either order:
      a. standing
      b. permanent
1.30 temporary
1.31 Either order:
      a. judge or interpret the meaning of the law
      b. punish those who break the law
1.32 Either order:
      a. civil cases
      b. criminal cases
1.33 disputes between two or more individuals
1.34 a person on trial who is accused of breaking
      a state law
1.35 Either order:
      a. felonies
      b. misdemeanors
1.36 a. three to nine
      b. seven
1.37 Any order:
      a. traffic violations
      b. disorderly conduct
      c. violation of health laws
1.38 state supreme court

1.39 Any order:
   a. burglary
   b. murder
   c. kidnapping
1.40 a. elected
   b. appointed
1.41 eight or ten
1.42 Rhode Island
1.43 courts of record
1.44 elected
1.45 Either order:
   a. jury
   b. trial judge
1.46 county courts
1.47 Either answer:
   district court *or* circuit court
1.48 Any order:
   a. appellate courts
   b. superior courts
   c. courts of common place
1.49 Any order:
   a. magistrate courts
   b. police courts
   c. municipal courts
1.50 All cases are heard by the judge, not by a trial jury.
1.51 a. hear traffic violations
   b. hear cases involving family disputes, separation of married couples, divorce cases and neglect of children
   c. hear cases involving young persons under 18 years of age
1.52 e
1.53 d
1.54 c
1.55 e
1.56 b
1.57 d
1.58 a
1.59 f
1.60 d
1.61 c
1.62 Teacher check
1.63 a
1.64 d
1.65 e
1.66 g
1.67 f
1.68 h
1.69 b
1.70 a
1.71 c
1.72 b
1.73 h

1.74 i *or* d
1.75 g
1.76 Examples; any order:
   a. highways
   b. health
   c. education
   d. hospitals
   e. public welfare
   f. insurance trusts
   or retirement of employees, public safety, prisons, natural resources, interest and debt redemption, service to veterans
1.77 Any order:
   a. general sales and property taxes
   b. oil, gas, alcoholic beverage, tobacco taxes
   c. motor-vehicle licenses
   d. individual and corporate income taxes
   e. inheritance and gift taxes
   f. the use of natural resources
1.78 Any order:
   a. life
   b. liberty
   c. property
1.79 Either order:
   a. birth certificate
   b. marriage license
1.80 false
1.81 false
1.82 true
1.83 false
1.84 true
1.85 d
1.86 e
1.87 b
1.88 c
1.89 a
1.90 Any order:
   a. federal
   b. state
   c. local
1.91 paying taxes
1.92 false
1.93 true
1.94 true
1.95 true
1.96 false
1.97 d
1.98 e
1.99 a
1.100 b
1.101 c

SELF TEST 1

1.01 10th
1.02 Any order:
    a. issue money
    b. establish an army
    c. regulate trade
1.03 two legislative branches
1.04 Either order:
    a. civil
    b. criminal
1.05 Secretary of State
1.06 a. 25
    b. United States
    c. state and district they represent
1.07 false
1.08 true
1.09 false
1.010 true
1.011 false
1.012 false
1.013 true
1.014 true
1.015 false
1.016 true
1.017 b
1.018 d
1.019 c
1.020 e
1.021 a
1.022 a
1.023 d
1.024 c
1.025 d
1.026 c
1.027 Any order:
    a. district or circuit courts
    b. appellate courts
    c. county courts
    d. superior courts
    or courts of common pleas,
    courts of records
1.028 a. hear traffic violations
    b. hear cases involving family disputes,
    separation of married couples, divorce
    cases, and neglect of children
    c. hear cases involving young persons
    under 18 years of age
1.029 Any order:
    a. general sales and property taxes or
    individual and corporate income taxes
    b. oil, gas, tobacco, alcoholic beverage taxes;
    inheritance or gift taxes
    c. motor-vehicle licenses or use of natural
    resources

SECTION 2

2.1 Jamestown
2.2 Either order:
    a. federal
    b. state
2.3 state government
2.4 Any order:
    a. county
    b. city
    c. town
    d. village
    e. township
2.5 a. legislature
    b. constitution
2.6 parishes
2.7 a. 254
    b. 3
2.8 San Francisco
2.9 taxes
2.10 elections
2.11 laws
2.12 services
2.13 false
2.14 true
2.15 false
2.16 false
2.17 true
2.18 d
2.19 e
2.20 b
2.21 c
2.22 county board
2.23 sheriff
2.24 constables
2.25 justice of the peace
2.26 township
2.27 false
2.28 true
2.29 false
2.30 false
2.31 false
2.32 c
2.33 e
2.34 d
2.35 b
2.36 a
2.37 false
2.38 true
2.39 true
2.40 false
2.41 true

SELF TEST 2

2.01 Either order:
a. federal
b. state
2.02 Any order:
a. boundaries
b. forms
c. powers
2.03 county board
2.04 welfare
2.05 Either order:
a. state
b. national
2.06 one person
or an executive
2.07 true
2.08 false
2.09 true
2.010 false
2.011 true
2.012 true
2.013 true
2.014 false
2.015 true
2.016 true
2.017 d
2.018 b
2.019 e
2.020 a
2.021 c
2.022 b
2.023 d
2.024 a
2.025 c
2.026 b
2.027 a
2.028 c
2.029 b
2.030 c
2.031 e
2.032 d
2.033 b
2.034 a
2.035 Any order:
a. general sales and property taxes
b. inheritance and gift taxes
c. motor-vehicle licenses
d. individual and corporate income taxes
e. oil, gas, liquor, beer, and tobacco taxes
f. use of natural resources

SECTION 3

3.1 Either order:
a. village
b. town
3.2 Either order:
a. fire
b. police
3.3 state legislature
3.4 false
3.5 true
3.6 true
3.7 true
3.8 false
3.9 c
3.10 e
3.11 a
3.12 b
3.13 d
3.14 Either order:
a. select
b. common
3.15 law-making
3.16 officials
3.17 false
3.18 false
3.19 true
3.20 false
3.21 false
3.22 d
3.23 a
3.24 e
3.25 c
3.26 b
3.27 high cost of living, crime rate, and deteriorating of buildings
3.28 rural areas
3.29 true
3.30 false
3.31 false
3.32 true
3.33 true
3.34 e
3.35 a
3.36 c
3.37 b
3.38 d

SELF TEST 3

3.01 Any order:
a. mayor-council
b. commission
c. city council-manager

3.02 Any order:
a. clerk
b. treasurer
c. attorney
or street commissioner, constable, board of health director

3.03 chief executive

3.04 expand

3.05 Either order:
a. expressways
b. parkways

3.06 parishes

3.07 thirty

3.08 Any order:
a. issue money
b. establish an army
c. regulate trade

3.09 Either order:
a. federal
b. state

3.010 enforce the law

3.011 money

3.012 state

3.013 governor

3.014 Any order:
a. executive
b. legislative
c. judicial

3.015 false

3.016 true

3.017 false

3.018 true

3.019 true

3.020 false

3.021 true

3.022 true

3.023 false

3.024 false

3.025 c

3.026 a

3.027 e

3.028 b

3.029 d

3.030 a

3.031 d

3.032 c

3.033 e

3.034 c

LIFEPAC TEST

1. Any order:
   a. federal
   b. state
   c. local
2. Any order:
   a. issue money
   b. establish an army
   c. regulate trade
3. Any order:
   a. boundaries
   b. forms
   c. ¬powers
4. Either order:
   a. state
   b. national
5. Either order:
   a. villages
   b. towns
6. Either order:
   a. select
   b. common
7. true
8. true
9. true
10. false
11. true
12. true
13. false
14. false
15. false
16. true
17. false
18. true
19. true
20. true
21. false
22. d
23. h
24. b
25. j
26. a
27. e
28. c
29. i
30. g
31. f
32. d
33. c
34. c
35. b
36. e
37. b
38. b
39. c
40. a
41. d

ALTERNATE LIFEPAC TEST

1.	bicameral	32.	b
2.	Any order:	33.	d
	a. lower state courts	34.	d
	b. state trials courts	35.	b
	c. higher state courts	36.	c
3.	Either order:	37.	d
	a. birth certificates	38.	b
	b. marriage licenses	39.	d
4.	Any order:	40.	c
	a. life	41.	a
	b. liberty	42.	c
	c. property		
5.	Any order:		
	a. mayor-council		
	b. commission		
	c. city manager		
6.	Either order:		
	a. expressways		
	b. parkways		
7.	suburbs		
	or rural areas		
8.	false		
9.	true		
10.	true		
11.	true		
12.	false		
13.	true		
14.	true		
15.	false		
16.	true		
17.	false		
18.	true		
19.	true		
20.	false		
21.	true		
22.	true		
23.	i		
24.	e		
25.	k		
26.	f		
27.	a		
28.	c		
29.	j		
30.	d		
31.	g		

HISTORY & GEOGRAPHY 903

ALTERNATE LIFEPAC TEST

NAME _____

DATE _____

SCORE _____

80

100

Complete these sentences (each answer, 3 points).

1. When a legislature has two branches, it is called a(n) _____ legislature.

2. The three types of courts found in most states are a. _____ ,
   b. _____ , and c. _____ .

3. Two documents accepted from one state to another are a. _____ ,
   and b. _____ .

4. The state constitution lists from its Bill of Rights the rights of a. _____ ,
   b. _____ , and c. _____ .

5. Three forms of city government are the a. _____ ,
   b. _____ , and c. _____ .

6. To alleviate transportation problems, many large cities built a. _____
   and b. _____ .

7. Many people are leaving the city and are moving to the _____ .

Answer *true* **or** *false* (each answer, 1 point).

8. _____ The responsible citizen does not necessarily know their representatives.

9. _____ In a democratic form of government such as ours, we have a checks and
   balances system.

10. _____ All laws protect each citizen the same way.

11. _____ One of the qualifications of a senator is that they are a citizen of the state.

12. _____ The state supreme court handles civil and criminal cases.

13. _____ County government supervises elections.

14. _____ County governments get their authority from the states.

15. _____ The county clerk keeps only records of county board actions.

16. _____ Counties in the states vary in number.

17. _____ The first local government in the United States began in Jamestown, New York.

18. _____ The mayor-council type of government is the oldest kind of city government.

19. _____ Many people believe that the metropolitan areas will continue to grow.

20. _____ Today the center of activity is in the center of large cities.

21. _____ Crime has been a cause of many people leaving the cities.

22. _____ We have a very affluent society.

Match these items (each answer, 2 points).

23. _____ appellate

24. _____ locales

25. _____ exofficio

26. _____ parish

27. _____ influx

28. _____ suburbs

29. _____ incorporated

30. _____ concurrent

31. _____ alleviate

32. _____ charter

a. coming in without stopping

b. plan of government

c. a district on the city's outskirts

d. acting together

e. places of residence

f. a district like a country

g. to make easier

h. a type of vote

i. higher court

j. bring together in a single whole

k. nonvoting member

Write the letter for the correct answer on each line (each answer, 2 points).

33. A good citizen will _____ .
    a. obey all laws
    b. let their representatives know about governmental problems
    c. support governmental work
    d. a, b, and c

34. The highest court in the state is the _____ .
    a. state trial court   b. lower state court
    c. higher state trial court   d. state supreme court

35. The sheriff _____ .
    a. records deaths in their district   b. carries out court orders
    c. collects traffic fines   d. raises taxes

36. The official who represents the state government in county trials is the _____ .
    a. county supervisor   b. sheriff
    c. district attorney   d. police chief

37. Counties provide for _____ .
    a. zoning   b. public education
    c. roads   d. a, b, and c

38. Local government gets its authority from the _____ government.
    a. federal   b. state
    c. county   d. city

39. A member of the council in an incorporated village may serve as _____ .
    a. clerk   b. treasurer
    c. attorney   d. street commissioner

40. In many of our metropolitan areas children have to play _____ .
    a. in parks   b. in playgrounds
    c. in streets   d. none of these

41. Under the commission plan a _____ controls the city government.
    a. number of people   b. mayor
    c. president   d. jury

42. Large cities can expand through _____ .
    a. suburbs   b. rural areas
    c. annexation   d. elections

HISTORY & GEOGRAPHY 904

Unit 4: Planning a Career

TEACHER NOTES

MATERIALS NEEDED FOR LIFEPAC	
Required	Suggested
None	None

ADDITIONAL LEARNING ACTIVITIES

Section 1: What a Career Is

1. Discuss the differences between: a *career* and a *job*, a *production industry* and a *service industry*, a *church-related occupation* and a *secular occupation*.

2. God has a plan for everyone's life. Ask students: Have you seen any part of God's plan for your own life? What do you think it is?

3. Instruct students to examine the list of occupations under Activity 1.15 of the LIFEPAC, and then choose (in order of preference) the three that would be the best fit. Have students explain their choices to a friend.

4. Assign students to write a short report on the job or career of a parent or family friend. The report should include what their responsibilities are, how they spend their day, how they feel about their work, and so on. How they would improve their job might also be included.

5. Discuss the following: What do missionaries do? Would you like to be one? Would you be willing to make the sacrifices in time, comfort, and money that would be necessary?

Section 2: How a Career Is Selected

1. Prompt groups to discuss the various jobs and careers available in your city or town, and evaluate one another's strengths and weaknesses for types of positions.

2. Instruct students to make a list of their special talents and interests. Ask, could these qualities help you in a future choice of a job or career?

Section 3: What Career Preparation Is Necessary

1. Have a local personnel manager or someone in charge of hiring for a large business or store speak to the class about what he or she looks for in a job applicant. Try to leave time for students' questions.

2. As a class, look at the job application in the LIFEPAC or find some examples of online job applications. Discuss the process: Why is so much information requested? Is it fair for a potential employer to ask so many questions? Have the students fill out the application to the best of their ability.

3. Have students conduct an imaginary job interview with a classmate, demonstrating the good and bad points listed in the LIFEPAC. When one person has been the "interviewer" and one the "applicant," conduct another session with the roles reversed.

4. Tell students to make a list of the goals they have set for themselves so far in life. Students should include the Christian goals that they think God expects.

5. Have students look at the job listings a recent local newspaper or search for local job openings online. Instruct them to choose any three job ads they would apply for if they were out of school and looking for work. Discuss: Are you surprised at the choices you made? Why, or why not?

Administer the LIFEPAC Test

The test is to be administered in one session. Give no help except with directions.
Evaluate the tests and review areas where the students have done poorly.
Review the pages and activities that stress the concepts tested.
If necessary, administer the Alternate LIFEPAC Test.

ANSWER KEYS

SECTION 1

1.1 Any order:
   a. a calling
   b. a lifework
   c. a service to others
   d. a divine plan for one's life

1.2 One's advancement or achievement in a particular occupation or lifework.

1.3 One's advancement or achievement in an occupation to which God called him.

1.4 Any order:
   a. instruct
   b. teach
   c. guide

1.5 true

1.6 true

1.7 false

1.8 false

1.9 specialization

1.10 Any order; examples:
   a. telephone
   b. electric light
   c. automobile
   or telegraph, cotton gin, steam power

1.11 service

1.12 God

1.13 Any order; examples:
   a. pony express
   b. stagecoach driver
   c. telegrapher

1.14 Any order; examples:
   a. gas station operator
   b. auto mechanic
   c. taxi driver
   d. farmer

1.15
   a. s
   b. s
   c. p
   d. s
   e. p
   f. s
   g. p
   h. s
   i. s
   j. p
   k. p
   l. s
   m. p
   n. s
   o. s
   p. s
   q. p, s
   r. s
   s. s
   t. s
   u. s
   v. p
   w. p
   x. s
   y. p, s
   z. s
   aa. s
   bb. s, p

1.16 Down
   1. guidance
   2. apprentice
   4. missionary
   5. career
   Across
   3. dedication
   6. specialization
   7. diversity

1.17
   a. moral purity or sanctification
   b. thankfulness
   c. let all things be done in charity
   d. obey and honor parents
   e. working and giving instead of stealing
   f. repent and trust Christ for salvation

1.18 Any order:
   a. what the Bible says – conscience
   b. how you feel – desire
   c. inner peace – sense of calm and rightness
   d. one's ability with God's power – freedom
   e. circumstances – open and closed doors

1.19 be saved

1.20 Either order:
   a. Paul
   b. Jeremiah

1.21 Any order:
   a. good
   b. acceptable
   c. perfect

1.22 lamp
   or light

1.23 true

1.24 false

1.25 true

1.26 false

1.27 true

1.28 d
1.29 e
1.30 a
1.31 c
1.32 b
1.33 Guidance is trusting God to give a person wisdom according to His Word; to make reasonable decisions under His control, in love, and for His glory.

SELF TEST 1

1.01 false
1.02 true
1.03 false
1.04 true
1.05 true
1.06 true
1.07 true
1.08 true
1.09 false
1.010 true
1.011 true
1.012 e
1.013 c
1.014 b
1.015 a
1.016 d
1.017 b
1.018 f
1.019 g
1.020 k
1.021 h
1.022 e
1.023 d
1.024 j
1.025 i
1.026 a
1.027 a. listening
        b. willing
1.028 faith
1.029 Any order:
        a. thankful
        b. obedient to parents
        c. hardworking
1.030 Either order:
        a. Jeremiah
        b. Paul
1.031 wait
1.032 a. feet
        b. path
1.033 p
1.034 s
1.035 s
1.036 s
1.037 s
1.038 p
1.039 p
1.040 s
1.041 p
1.042 Guidance is trusting God to give a person wisdom according to His Word; to make reasonable decisions under His control, in love, and for His glory.

1.043 Hint:
First, I would read the Bible daily and ask God to guide me. Then I would consider my abilities, what I like, whether circumstances seem favorable, and whether I feel right about choosing a particular career.

SECTION 2

2.1	d
2.2	b
2.3	i
2.4	h
2.5	l
2.6	a
2.7	c
2.8	b
2.9	k
2.10	l
2.11	e
2.12	f
2.13	f, h
2.14	c, a
2.15	g
2.16	i
2.17	false
2.18	true
2.19	true
2.20	true
2.21	false

2.22 Examples:
supervises, bookkeeping

2.23 Examples:
construct, blueprints

2.24 Examples:
correspondence, appointments

2.25 Examples:
prevention, reforestation

2.26 Examples:
transport, destinations

2.27 Examples:
prescriptions, treatment

2.28 Examples:
hand tools, welds

2.29 Examples:
examine, research

2.30 Example:
repairs

2.31 Examples:
sells, merchandise

2.32 Examples:
human beings, culture

2.33 Examples:
designs, information

2.34 Teacher check

2.35 People Skills; any order:
a. health
b. sales
c. social sciences
d. other professions
e. business administration

Thing Skills; any order:
f. building trades
g. driving
h. manual
i. math and science
j. mechanics and repairmen
k. clerical
l. conservation

2.36 Either order:
a. driving – I enjoy moving around and seeing different things.
b. other professions – I like working with people.

2.37 f
2.38 b
2.39 g
2.40 k
2.41 a
2.42 d
2.43 h
2.44 i
2.45 c
2.46 e
2.47 Examples:
A – English
B – math
C – science
A – home economic
B – history and geography
A – physical education
B – art
C – industrial arts
2.48 Example:
a. English
b. P.E.
2.49 Example:
 X sports
 X speech
 X student government
 X other – yearbook editor
2.50 Example:
a. clerical
b. other professions
2.51 Example:
 X fishing
 X cooking
 X model building
 X other – travel, visiting friends, shopping
2.52 Example:
a. sales
b. health

2.53 Example:
a. a baseball player
b. Baseball players made a lot of money and were well-known.
2.54 Examples:
a. minister – can help people
b. locomotive engineer – can go places; gives feeling of power
c. chemist – gets good pay; science is interesting
2.55 Example:
locomotive engineer – parents didn't favor it
2.56 Examples:
teaching – security; college needed
minister – think I have the calling
2.57 Examples:
a. customs man   would not like
b. traveling salesman   would not like
c. postal driver   would like
2.58 Example:
college professor at a Christian school could combine Scripture with teaching
2.59 Examples:
a. yes – bridge operator
b. yes – librarian
c. yes – store clerk
d. yes – politician
e. yes – teacher
f. yes – repairman
g. no
h. yes – lawyer
i. no
j. yes – illustrator
k. yes – deliveryman
l. no
m. yes – mail carrier
n. yes – stenographer
o. no
p. yes – stewardess
q. yes – accountant
r. yes – banker
s. yes – nurse
t. yes – writer
u. no
v. yes – store clerk
w. yes – real estate salesman
x. yes – lawyer
y. no
z. no
aa. no
bb. yes – salesman
cc. yes – acting
dd. yes – comedian
ee. no

2.60 Examples:
  _X_ paint or draw pictures
  _X_ take photographs
  _X_ write short stories
  _X_ act in a play
  _X_ advise people with problems
  _X_ decorate a house
  _X_ write articles giving ideas
  _X_ instruct students
  _X_ inspect working conditions
  _X_ conduct experiments
  _X_ program a computer
  _X_ operate office machines
  _X_ deliver merchandise
  _X_ make change with money
  _X_ serve food and drinks
  _X_ sell tickets
  _X_ repair engines
  _X_ drive a bus
  _X_ repair TV's
  _X_ letter posters
  _X_ bake pastries
  _X_ straighten bent fenders
  _X_ make lab tests
  _X_ plan menus
  _X_ report the weather
  _X_ supervise factory workers
  _X_ type letters
  _X_ be a model
  _X_ pump gas
  _X_ do hair styling
  _X_ use drills and lathes
  _X_ frame houses
  _X_ pack vegetables

2.61 Teacher check

SELF TEST 2

2.01 true
2.02 true
2.03 false
2.04 true
2.05 true
2.06 false
2.07 true
2.08 false
2.09 false
2.010 true
2.011 true
2.012 false
2.013 true
2.014 true
2.015 false
2.016 c
2.017 b
2.018 a
2.019 a
2.020 b
2.021 k
2.022 c
2.023 f
2.024 g
2.025 j
2.026 e
2.027 b
2.028 a
2.029 h
2.030 i
2.031 thing skills
2.032 people skills
2.033 thing skills
2.034 thing skills
2.035 people skills
2.036 Across
  1. delinquency
  3. premium
  4. statistics
  6. dictation
  8. receipt
  9. voucher
  Down
  2. correspondence
  3. prescription
  5. audit
  7. juvenile
2.037 lifework
2.038 one hundred
2.039 specialization
2.040 a. service
  b. production

SECTION 3

3.1	false
3.2	false
3.3	true
3.4	true
3.5	false
3.6	true
3.7	true
3.8	false
3.9	false
3.10	true

3.11 Any order:
   a. telephone
   b. yard care
   c. garbage
   d. electricity
   e. upkeep
   f. insurance

3.12	f
3.13	b
3.14	d
3.15	e
3.16	d, j
3.17	b, a
3.18	d, j, e
3.19	a, b, f
3.20	f
3.21	g, i
3.22	a, e
3.23	h, a, i
3.24	c
3.25	g
3.26	i, g
3.27	k, c
3.28	g, b
3.29	i, h
3.30	b, f
3.31	d, j, e
3.32	i, h, k
3.33	d, j, e
3.34	one's attitude

3.35 Any order:
   a. God has forgiven the beliver's sins.
   b. They are a child of God.
   c. God lives in their life.

3.36	c
3.37	b
3.38	a
3.39	d

3.40 Any order:
   a. accept an available job
   b. attend junior college
   c. enter a trade
   d. attend a public four-year college or university
   e. attend a private four-year college or university
   f. take a specialized course
   g. attend a Christian college
   h. enter the military

3.41 Any order:
   a. ask friends
   b. review online and print ads
   c. contacts businesses/fill out applications
   d. search Indeed and LinkedIn
   e. watch stores windows
   f. contact temp agency
   or employment placement service

3.42	false
3.43	false
3.44	false
3.45	false
3.46	true
3.47	true
3.48	false
3.49	true
3.50	false
3.51	false
3.52	true
3.53	true

3.54 Any order:
   a. honest
   b. likeable
   c. intelligent

3.55	do
3.56	don't
3.57	don't
3.58	do
3.59	don't
3.60	don't
3.61	don't
3.62	do
3.63	do
3.64	don't
3.65	do
3.66	c
3.67	e
3.68	f
3.69	b

SELF TEST 3

3.01   true
3.02   false
3.03   false
3.04   true
3.05   true
3.06   false
3.07   true
3.08   true
3.09   true
3.010 false
3.011 b
3.012 a
3.013 c
3.014 a
3.015 b
3.016 b
3.017 a
3.018 c
3.019 d
3.020 c
3.021 a
3.022 d
3.023 c
3.024 a
3.025 a
3.026 b
3.027 c
3.028 d
3.029 a
3.030 c
3.031 a
3.032 a
3.033 c
3.034 b
3.035 a
3.036 Christian
3.037 dedication
3.038 missionary
3.039 trust
3.040 industrialization
3.041 guidance
3.042 service
3.043 career area
3.044 career
3.045 service

LIFEPAC TEST

1.	d	**29.**	k, l
2.	j	**30.**	c
3.	g	**31.**	k
4.	a	**32.**	a
5.	k	**33.**	f
6.	h	**34.**	l
7.	f	**35.**	e
8.	i	**36.**	l
9.	c	**37.**	i
10.	b	**38.**	b
11.	true	**39.**	h
12.	true	**40.**	j
13.	false	**41.**	d
14.	true	**42.**	e
15.	true	**43.**	g
16.	false		
17.	true		
18.	false		
19.	false		
20.	false		

21. Any order:
   a. what the Bible says
   b. inner peace
   c. personal ability
   d. circumstances

22. a. wisdom
   b. reasonable decisions
   c. love
   d. glory

23. a. friends
   b. business
   or read newspaper ads,
      watch store windows,
      visit state employment office,
      put an ad in the paper,
      write companies,
      call local companies,
      fill out applications,
      see personnel managers

24. b
25. c
26. b
27. c
28. c

ALTERNATE LIFEPAC TEST

1. true
2. false
3. true
4. false
5. true
6. true
7. false
8. false
9. true
10. true
11. d
12. f
13. a
14. g
15. k
16. b
17. j
18. h
19. c
20. i
21. c
22. b
23. a
24. b
25. b
26. c
27. a
28. d
29. c
30. c
31. Examples:
    a. factory worker
    or farmer
    b. minister
    or doctor
32. God
33. Examples; either order:
    a. ability
    b. circumstances
34. agree
35. agree
36. agree
37. agree
38. disagree
39. Any order:
    a. be early
    b. know something about the company
    c. smile
    d. look interviewer in the eye
    e. be rested and alert

HISTORY & GEOGRAPHY 904

ALTERNATE LIFEPAC TEST

NAME _____

DATE _____

SCORE _____

68

85

Answer *true* **or** *false* (each answer, 1 point).

1. _____ A career requires a person's full-time dedication.

2. _____ God expects us to choose a career on our own.

3. _____ The Bible gives specific directions regarding God's will.

4. _____ Choosing a career is comparatively easy because of the limited number of jobs.

5. _____ The mathematics and science career area could include bridge designing.

6. _____ Career areas are groups of jobs with similar functions or skills.

7. _____ Achievement in school has little to do with career selection.

8. _____ Christian values such as honesty and cooperation are not needed in the secular world of work.

9. _____ Honoring the Lord and pleasing others should be a Christian's highest goals.

10. _____ The state employment office is one source of job openings.

Match these items (each answer, 2 points).

11. _____ service job

12. _____ initiative

13. _____ conscience

14. _____ Jeremiah

15. _____ wisdom

16. _____ building trades

17. _____ birthday gifts

18. _____ dependability

19. _____ reference

20. _____ attitude

a. what the Bible says

b. a career area

c. something asked on a job application

d. teaching

e. young; youthful

f. a Christian value important to an employer

g. person who knew God's plan for his life

h. a Christian value meaning that someone can be counted on

i. the key factor in job success or failure

j. personal expenses

k. God promises this

Write the letter for the correct answer on each line (each answer, 2 points).

21. God promises to _____ those who ask Him.
    a. give wisdom to
    b. guide
    c. both a and b
    d. ignore

22. Firefighters are _____ .
    a. production workers
    b. service workers
    c. always volunteers
    d. state officials

23. The number of jobs open to a person in the United States is more than _____ .
    a. 20,000
    b. 30,000
    c. 10,000
    d. 100,00

24. You can begin developing your job abilities by _____ .
    a. watching television
    b. working hard in school
    c. ignoring your parents' requests
    d. buying a car

25. When applying for a job, you should _____ .
    a. dress sloppily
    b. smile
    c. talk softly
    d. not worry about whether the information on your application is accurate

26. Nursing belongs to the _____ career area.
    a. manual
    b. clerical
    c. health
    d. occupational

27. Selling goods in a store belongs to the _____ career area.
    a. sales
    b. clerical
    c. scientific
    d. business administration

28. During a job interview a person should _____ the interviewer.
    a. laugh at
    b. stare at
    c. flatter
    d. be courteous to

29. Learning about one's employer and supporting him is _____ .
    a. blind obedience
    b. following directions
    c. loyalty
    d. unwise

30. A high school graduate has _____ career opportunities open to him or her.
    a. one
    b. two
    c. several
    d. no

Complete these sentences (each answer, 3 points).

31. An example of a production job is a. _____ and
    an example of a service job is b. _____ .

32. The One who knows someone's abilities and potential is _____ .

33. Besides the Bible, your own desires, and inner peace, two other factors to consider in God's
    guidance are a. _____ and b. _____ .

Write *agree* **or** *disagree* **before each statement** (each answer, 1 point).

34. _____ Your interests can be an important clue as to what career you should choose.

35. _____ More people work in serving people than in producing goods.

36. _____ The Bible is like a lamp because it sheds light on how Christians should live.

37. _____ Some occupations require more skill in handling things than people.

38. _____ An interviewer does not like to hear the applicant use the interviewer's name.

Complete this activity (each answer, 3 points).

39.   List five things to remember while interviewing for jobs.

a. _____

b. _____

c. _____

d. _____

e. _____

HISTORY & GEOGRAPHY 905

Unit 5: Citizenship

TEACHER NOTES

MATERIALS NEEDED FOR LIFEPAC	
Required	Suggested
None	• copy of the United States Constitution • reference books or online sources

ADDITIONAL LEARNING ACTIVITIES

Section 1: Acquisition of Citizenship

1. As a class, make a chart that shows (through pictures or drawings) how a person becomes a citizen of the United States.

2. Bring to class and discuss with students specific cases of people in the past and present who have lost citizenship. Be sure students understand the reasons for the loss of citizenship.

3. Invite a recently naturalized citizen to class to discuss their experiences in becoming a citizen of the United States.

4. Have students create a play or story that includes the process of citizenship (or includes someone who loses citizenship).

5. Direct students to investigate the specific procedures a person must go through to become a citizen in your state, and then share the information as a class. Find out when individuals can be awarded citizenship and attend the event if it is nearby.

6. Have students research statistics on the number of people who have lost citizenship and for what reasons they lost citizenship.

7. Assign students to research and do a report or paper on the case of Wong Kim Ark.

Section 2: Rights of Citizenship

1. As a class, make a chart or bulletin board display to illustrate the First Amendment rights, the personal rights, and the property rights of the Constitution.

2. Explain to students through specific examples exactly what rights, privileges, and immunities of the Constitution and citizenship mean to them personally.

3. Have a group discussion in which you relate the specific rights, privileges, and immunities to specific incidents in which you might be involved as a minor or as an adult.

4. Have the class examine a copy of your state constitution. Discuss together: Does it provide for the same rights, privileges, and immunities as the United States Constitution? If it does not, do you maintain the rights guaranteed in the United States Constitution? Have groups report to the class, or have a group debate on the subject.

5. Have the class Investigate or research the Supreme Court decision on prayer and Bible reading in the public schools. Assign students to write a report agreeing with or opposing the Supreme Court position.

6. Have students research and present costs or rules that apply to nonresidents of your state that do not apply to residents.

Section 3: Responsibilities of Citizenship

1. Have students explain the structure, philosophies, and candidate success records of the major political parties. Then, have them apply the explanation to the state as well as to national politics.

2. Bring to class examples of written literature designed to keep people informed in the political and governmental process. As a class, discuss reliable and unreliable sources of information.

3. Arrange to visit a polling place during an election or visit the board of elections. Have the people in charge explain the voting process, voting machine use, or ballot use if that is common in your locality. Ask them to explain how one registers to vote and how ballots are counted after an election. Ask, also, about your state's voting requirements.

4. Ask a local, state, or national politician to speak to the class about the political process and how students and adults can become involved.

5. Assign students to write a letter or send an email to a public official, telling them about a situation that needs correcting, complimenting them on a particular vote on legislation, or asking questions about something important.

6. If possible, arrange for students to attend a meeting of a local political party to learn the concerns of that group. Have the students in attendance relate their experiences to the class.

Administer the LIFEPAC Test

The test is to be administered in one session. Give no help except with directions.
Evaluate the tests and review areas where the students have done poorly.
Review the pages and activities that stress the concepts tested.
If necessary, administer the Alternate LIFEPAC Test.

ANSWER KEYS

SECTION 1

1.1 Citizenship means full membership in a political community.

1.2
a. persons who have immigrated to this country, but not obtained citizenship; foreigners temporarily residing in this country; representatives of foreign governments
b. persons who owe allegiance to this country, are protected by it, but lack some privileges of citizenship

1.3 Fourteenth Amendment

1.4 right of the soil

1.5 place of birth

1.6 right of blood

1.7 parentage

1.8 It established the principle of *jus soli* for the United States, defines the limits of that principle, and provides protection against a citizen being deprived of their birthright.

1.9 Any person domiciled in the United States is subject to the jurisdiction of the United States.

1.10 Any order:
a. in the United States
b. in the District of Columbia
c. in Puerto Rico
or the Virgin Islands; Guam; a United States vessel; public vessel in United States territorial waters

1.11 Any order:
a. if born of parents both of whom are United States citizens and one has residence in United States
b. if born in American outlying possession where one parent is a citizen and lived in United States one year
c. if born of noncitizen and citizen parents, where citizen has lived in United States for one year
or if born of alien and citizen parents, where citizen has lived in United States for ten years, five after age fourteen, and child lives in United States for five years between ages fourteen and twenty-eight; if found in United States under five years of age of unknown parentage and not shown to have been born out of this country before reaching twenty-one years of age

1.12 false

1.13 true

1.14 true

1.15 false

1.16 true

1.17 establishing a person as if they were a native; granting a person citizenship

1.18 Immigration and Naturalization Service

1.19 the McCarran Act (Immigration and Nationality Act of 1952)

1.20 c

1.21 b

1.22 d

1.23 a

1.24
a. 5
b. 3
c. 6
d. 2
e. 4
f. 1

1.25 Teacher check

1.26 Either order:
a. if they are shown to have concealed material, facts, or misrepresented themself in acquiring citizenship
b. if they take up permanent residence in a foreign country within five years of naturalization
or if they affiliate with a subversive group within five years of naturalization; if they refuse to testify to congressional committee about alleged subversive activities within ten years of naturalization

1.27 Any order:
a. formally renounce United States citizenship
b. obtain naturalization in foreign country
c. take oath of allegiance to foreign country
d. serve in foreign armed forces without United States approval
or vote in foreign election; serve in foreign government

1.28 false

1.29 false

1.30 false

1.31 false

1.32 Teacher check

SELF TEST 1

1.01 c
1.02 b
1.03 f
1.04 c
1.05 a
1.06 a
1.07 b
1.08 e
1.09 a
1.010 c
1.011 d
1.012 b
1.013 b
1.014 g
1.015 e
1.016 b
1.017 a
1.018 d
1.019 d
1.020 b
1.021 b
1.022 a. birth
 b. naturalization
1.023 Either order:
 a. legislative actions (group)
 b. individually
1.024 Fourteenth Amendment
1.025 domiciled in the United States
1.026 Any order:
 a. joining a subversive organization
 b. by failing to testify before a congressional committee concerning subversive activities
 or by taking up permanent residence in a foreign country
1.027 5
1.028 4
1.029 3
1.030 7
1.031 1
1.032 6
1.033 2
1.034 It establishes the principle of *jus soli* for the United States, defines the limits of that principle, and provides against a citizen being deprived of their birthright.
1.035 They can be born in a country recognizing *jus soli* of alien parents from a country recognizing *jus sanguinis*; or they can be a United States citizen, a state citizen.

1.036 They renounce United States citizenship; vote in foreign elections; serve in foreign government; serve in foreign armed forces without United States approval; take oath of allegiance to foreign country; obtain naturalization in foreign country.
1.037 They are naturalized; however, thousands obtain citizenship by *jus sanguinis*, and thousands of thousands by *jus soli*.

SECTION 2

2.1 First Amendment
2.2 No established church had a clear majority at the time of independence.
2.3 Time off during school to attend religious classes on a voluntary basis.
2.4 They believed saluting the flag was idolatry.
2.5 Through a suit, the Supreme Court declared that these activities were an infringement on religious freedom.
2.6 A right that relates to the essence of the right; for example, freedom of religion, speech, assembly.
2.7 Any order:
   a. religion
   b. speech
   c. assembly
2.8 clear and present danger
2.9 Any order:
   a. lewd, obscene
   b. libelous
   c. profane
   d. insulting or "fighting words"
2.10 to keep and bear arms
2.11 slavery
2.12 e
2.13 c
2.14 f
2.15 a
2.16 d
2.17 b
2.18 writ of habeas corpus
2.19 Any order:
   a. jury contains exactly twelve citizens
   b. trial supervised and instructed by judge
   c. verdict should be unanimous
2.20 unreasonable search and seizure
2.21 when a person is put on trial twice for the same offense
2.22 The court interpreted the clause as a procedural right at first, then changed within the past eighty years to interpreting it as a substantive right.
2.23 The phrase has never been satisfactorily defined, but it should include the provisions of the Sixth and Eighth Amendments.

2.24 false
2.25 true
2.26 false
2.27 false
2.28 true
2.29 false
2.30 false
2.31 true
2.32 false
2.33 Example:
   No one can claim the right against self-incrimination in God's judgment; the words have already been spoken and cannot be recalled; we shall give account of every idle word to God.
2.34 paramount ownership
2.35 The government has the property condemned; the court orders it sold; a fair value is appraised; the value is accepted by the court; the price is paid, the government takes title.
2.36 property used for illegal purposes; property seized through taxation; property loss through conditions of location
2.37 the Fourteenth Amendment
2.38 the Slaughter House Cases in 1873
2.39 national citizenship
2.40 b
2.41 d
2.42 Teacher check

SELF TEST 2

2.01	g
2.02	c
2.03	d
2.04	j
2.05	e
2.06	i
2.07	a
2.08	d
2.09	h
2.010	f
2.011	b
2.012	a
2.013	c
2.014	j
2.015	f
2.016	d
2.017	d
2.018	c
2.019	b
2.020	a
2.021	d

2.022 Any order:
a. freedom of religion
b. freedom of speech
c. freedom of assembly

2.023 Either order:
a. legislative action (group)
b. individually

2.024 "released time"

2.025 jurisdiction

2.026 freedom of speech

2.027 true

2.028 false

2.029 false

2.030 false

2.031 true

2.032 true

2.033 true

2.034 A right that relates to the essence of the right; for example, freedom of religion, speech, assembly.

2.035 A right that relates to a judicial or governmental process; for example, trial by jury.

2.036 No listing of privileges or immunities exists in any government document; Supreme Court cases have not been precise and unanimous in explaining privileges or immunities.

2.037 They gained citizenship either through individual naturalization, *jus soli* or *jus sanguinis*.

SECTION 3

3.1 Any order:
a. State of the Union address
b. on specific issues of national concern
c. periodic press conferences

3.2 Any order:
a. listening to presidential address
b. listening to congressional proceedings
c. listening to political commentators
d. attending meetings concerning public affairs
e. meeting politicians and elected officials
f. reading newspapers and political literature
g. listening to speakers from civic groups

3.3	b
3.4	d
3.5	a
3.6	d
3.7	d

3.8 a. Since dissent approves of government's authority but disapproves of government's action, these verses do not apply.
b. Since alienation disapproves of the authority of government and would abolish the government's authority, these verses condemn alienation.

3.9 Either order:
a. Republican
b. Democrat

3.10 to ensure that the party's candidates get elected so that government policy is directed by party beliefs

3.11 to purchase advertisement space and time

3.12 Example:
Teach people to use voting machine; help register delinquent votes; pass out literature.

3.13	d
3.14	a
3.15	c
3.16	b

3.17 Any order:
a. must be a United States citizen
b. must have residency in the state
c. must be registered to vote

3.18 Any order; example:
a. failure to register
b. lack of reliable information on candidates
c. intimidation by a social superior

3.19 Any order; example:
   a. legal restrictions, like residence requirements
   b. inclement weather that prevents access to polls
   c. illness or disability
3.20 3
3.21 2
3.22 1
3.23 6
3.24 4
3.25 7
3.26 8
3.27 5
3.28 Teacher check

SELF TEST 3

3.01 e
3.02 i
3.03 a
3.04 b
3.05 j
3.06 e
3.07 f
3.08 d
3.09 c
3.010 k
3.011 a
3.012 g
3.013 k
3.014 h
3.015 d
3.016 d
3.017 b
3.018 d
3.019 b
3.020 c
3.021 a
3.022 Fourteenth Amendment
3.023 Any order:
   a. freedom of religion
   b. freedom of speech
   c. freedom of assembly
3.024 expatriation
3.025 Any order:
   a. listening to presidential addresses
   b. listening to congressional proceedings
   c. listening to political commentators
   d. attending meetings concerning public affairs
   e. meeting politicians or elected officials
   or reading newspapers or political literature; listening to speakers from civic groups
3.026 false
3.027 true
3.028 true
3.029 true
3.030 Any order:
   a. must be a United States citizen
   b. must have residency in the state
   c. must be registered to vote
3.031 It establishes the principle of *jus soli* for the United States, defines the limits of that principle, and provides protection against a citizen being deprived of their birthright.
3.032 A right that relates to the essence of the right; for example, freedom of religion, speech, assembly.

3.033 Any order:
  a. they believed their vote would not be
      effective;
  b. they were intimidated;
  c. they did not register;
  d. the election was too complex;
  e. they did not establish residency;
  or illness;
      no transportation;
      inclement weather;
      lack of reliable information on candidates;
      little choice in candidate selection;
      voting is too difficult;
      political corruption

LIFEPAC TEST

1. f
2. p
3. j
4. h
5. r
6. k
7. u
8. q
9. i
10. w
11. o
12. b
13. g
14. d
15. n
16. a
17. v
18. l
19. t
20. m
21. d
22. b
23. b
24. d
25. b
26. d
27. a
28. 4
29. 6
30. 1
31. 5
32. 3
33. 2
34. false
35. true
36. true
37. true
38. true
39. true
40. true
41. true
42. *jus soli*
43. *jus sanguinis*
44. First Amendment
45. just compensation
46. treason
47. politics

ALTERNATE LIFEPAC TEST

1. c
2. e
3. h
4. j
5. f
6. a
7. i
8. b
9. d
10. g
11. false
12. true
13. false
14. true
15. true
16. true
17. true
18. true
19. false
20. false
21. Fourteenth
22. Either order:
    a. property used for illegal purposes
    b. for public use through taxation
23. Any order:
    a. initiative
    b. referendum
    c. recall
24. treason
25. twelve
26. to get its candidates elected
27. Fifth
28. d
29. c
30. b
31. b
32. c
33. a
34. d
35. a
36. b
37. c
38. 18 years of age; legally entered the country; 5 years continuous United States residency, and in the state where they petition for naturalization for six months; must speak, read, write, and understand English; have basic understanding of United States history and government; good moral character; attachment to the principles of the Constitution.

39. presidential addresses and news
    conferences; through the media;
    meetings on public affairs;
    civic group pamphlets;
    speakers at public meetings;
    discussing issues with politicians;
    observation of public bodies at meetings

HISTORY & GEOGRAPHY 905

ALTERNATE LIFEPAC TEST

NAME _____

DATE _____

SCORE _____

80

100

Match these items (each answer, 2 points).

1. _____ citizen

2. _____ McCarran-Walter Immigration and Nationality Act of 1952

3. _____ naturalization

4. _____ statelessness

5. _____ Weeks Case, 1914

6. _____ immunities

7. _____ Slaughter House Case

8. _____ platform

9. _____ property right guaranteed

10. _____ expatriation

a. privileges

b. position of a political party on matters concerning government problems

c. person born or naturalized in the United States and subject to its jurisdiction

d. Fifth Amendment

e. defines *jus soli* citizenship

f. established rule of evidence

g. forfeit of citizenship

h. establishing a person as if they were a native of the country

i. first court ruling on the meaning of privileges

j. without citizenship in any country

Answer *true* **or** *false* (each answer, 2 points).

11. _____ The right to possess firearms is guaranteed without restriction to all United States citizens.

12. _____ The prohibitions against *ex post facto* laws are confined to penal rather than civil laws.

13. _____ Through recall, a citizen may approve or reject a proposed statute.

14. _____ In the State of the Union message, the president of the United States gives their evaluation of the condition and position of the country.

15. _____ People born in a United States mission abroad whose parents are not United States citizens are United States citizens.

16. _____ People born in other countries may become naturalized citizens through a congressional action.

17. _____ A naturalized citizen may have their citizenship revoked if they affiliate with a subversive organization.

18. _____ A person must be a United States citizen before they can vote.

19. _____ The major reason many people do not vote is because they believe voting is too difficult.

20. _____ Representatives to Congress are elected to perpetuate their own interests on legislation.

Complete these sentences (each answer, 3 points).

21. The privileges or immunities a citizen enjoys when traveling abroad are extended to them through provisions of the _____ Amendment to the Constitution.

22. The occasions when national, state, or local governments may seize private property without compensation are a. _____ and b. _____ .

23. Three ways citizens may formally participate in their government are
a. _____ , b. _____ , and c. _____ .

24. The worst of all political crimes is _____ .

25. A jury usually consists of _____ people.

26. The primary goal of a political party is _____ .

27. The primary property right guaranteed in the Constitution is in the _____ Amendment.

Write the letter for the correct answer on each line (each answer, 2 points).

28. The right of a confined person to be shown if sufficient evidence exists for their continued
    confinement is _____ .
    a. Writ of mandamus   b. Nonconfinement law
    c. Writ of Assistance   d. Writ of Habeas Corpus

29. If the jury cannot reach a verdict, _____ .
    a. the judge decides whether the defendant is guilty or innocent
    b. the jurors deliberate until they reach a verdict
    c. the judge declares a mistrial
    d. the defendant is acquitted

30. In 1963, the Supreme Court ruled that requiring Bible reading in public schools is _____ .
    a. permitted
    b. an infringement upon the guarantees of freedom of religion
    c. permitted if students have the option of leaving the classroom during Bible reading
    d. part of the guarantee of freedom of religion

31. Trial by jury is a _____ right guaranteed by the Constitution.
    a. substantive   b. procedural
    c. personal   d. First Amendment

32. Before an agent of the government may search a person's property, the agent needs _____
    to search.
    a. to prove a crime   b. a good reason
    c. probable cause   d. no real reason

33. Which of the following items is not a voting requirement in all states? _____
    a. passing a literacy test
    b. United States citizenship
    c. residency in the state where the person wants to vote
    d. registration to vote

34. The Fifth Amendment protects the interests of the property owner in that they cannot be
    deprived of their property without _____ .
    a. their consent   b. condemnation proceedings
    c. a government transfer   d. due process of law

35. Double jeopardy applies to which of the following statements? _____
    a. A person is tried twice for the same offense.
    b. A person is released by authorities before they are indicted.
    c. The prosecutor voluntarily abandons their duties in the case.
    d. The jury cannot arrive at a unanimous verdict.

36. Which of the following statements is not a way a citizen may expatriate himself? _____
    a. Make a formal renunciation of United States citizenship.
    b. Leave the United States and live in another country.
    c. Serve in the government of a foreign state.
    d. Vote in a political election of a foreign state.

37. If a witness refuses to testify while under an order from a district judge while having

    immunity, they will be _____ .
    a. sent to prison   b. allowed to refuse to testify
    c. in contempt of court   d. prosecuted

Answer these questions (each answer, 5 points).

38. What are the requirements for individual naturalization?

    _____

    _____

    _____

    _____

    _____

39. How can a United States citizen keep well informed about the government?

    _____

    _____

    _____

    _____

    _____

HISTORY & GEOGRAPHY 906

Unit 6: The Earth and Man

TEACHER NOTES

MATERIALS NEEDED FOR LIFEPAC	
Required	Suggested
None	• wall map of the world • wall map of the Middle East showing ancient countries, cities, and topography of Abraham's time • reference books or online sources

ADDITIONAL LEARNING ACTIVITIES

Section 1: The Earth Is Man's Home

1. Discuss with students the responsibility in stewardship that man has toward God if one believes that God is the owner of all creation.

2. Discuss with students the three races of man that came forth from Noah's three sons.

3. Discuss with students in what way Noah was like a modern-day zookeeper.

4. Discuss with students the dividing line between prehistory and history.

5. Arrange a trip to a museum where you can see items of prehistoric interest.

6. Provide the following directions for research: Conduct a Bible search on longevity. Find the genealogies located in Genesis 5. Then find out the ages of the following people to see how long early man lived—Adam, Seth, Enos, Canaan, Mahalaleel, Jared, Enoch, Methuselah, Lamech. In addition, list the things that man had learned to do before the Flood.

7. Have students review or look up the five steps in the scientific method. Assign them to write a report or give an oral report in which they discuss evolution in relation to the steps of the scientific method.

Section 2: The Earth Is Developed by Man

1. Discuss with students the areas of the world where great population densities exist. Discuss with students the advantages, as well as the problems associated with great population density.

2. Discuss with students why civilizations developed in particular areas of the world. What factors contributed to the development?

3. Discuss with students the importance of navigation in modern society.

4. Invite an environmental expert or a geologist to speak to the class on natural resources, their importance in our lives, and what can occur as their supplies are depleted.

5. Arrange a visit to a museum that features early navigational equipment or a visit to a museum that features early industrial equipment.

6. Arrange a visit to a factory for a tour. Afterwards, have a class discussion on the adaptation of older methods of mass production that students saw in the visit.

7. Have students interview an elderly citizen in the community. Students should ask questions such as, "Did you grow up in a rural or urban area?" How many times and how far have you moved during your lifetime?" "What forms of transportation were common when you were young?" "How has industry changed during your lifetime?" "What kind of work did you do during your lifetime?" How much education was normal when you were of school age?" Have students report to the rest of the class.

8. Have the students research a problem that is directly related to the Industrial Revolution, and then write a report to explain the problem and give suggestions for its solution.

Section 3: The Earth Has a Future

1. Discuss with students the effect that governmental controls have on the Christian's desire to propagate the Gospel of Jesus Christ.

2. Discuss with students the effects of war on individual lives. If possible, invite a theologian to your class to discuss in more detail God's plan for man's eternal habitat.

3. Have a group discussion on the ways Christians may lead a Godly life in the face of world evils and in preparation for Christ's judgment.

4. Have students keep a current affairs notebook that includes items from news sources about the future of the earth and environment.

5. Arrange for students to interview a visiting missionary to learn about how the Gospel is being preached in other nations. Have students prepare a report to the class on the subject.

Administer the LIFEPAC Test

The test is to be administered in one session. Give no help except with directions.
Evaluate the tests and review areas where the students have done poorly.
Review the pages and activities that stress the concepts tested.
If necessary, administer the Alternate LIFEPAC Test.

ANSWER KEYS

SECTION 1

1.1	one large continent
1.2	Arizona
1.3	c
1.4	b
1.5	c
1.6	b
1.7	a
1.8	d
1.9	c
1.10	c
1.11	d
1.12	b
1.13	c
1.14	a
1.15	a
1.16	b
1.17	Fertile Crescent
1.18	Babel
1.19	language
1.20	confounded
1.21	Sumerians
1.22	Babylon
1.23	Ur
1.24	1400 B.C.
1.25	Any order:
	a. Japheth; Europe
	b. Ham; Africa
	c. Shem; China
1.26	true
1.27	true
1.28	true
1.29	false
1.30	true
1.31	true
1.32	Either order:
	a. Kish
	b. Nippur
1.33	Hammurabi
1.34	Hittites
1.35	Menes
1.36	Pharaohs
1.37	Memphis
1.38	hieroglyphics
1.39	Phoenicians
1.40	famine
1.41	Either order:
	a. Hebrew
	b. Arabic
1.42	Teacher check

SELF TEST 1

1.01	5
1.02	8
1.03	3
1.04	1
1.05	9
1.06	10
1.07	4
1.08	6
1.09	7
1.010	2
1.011	c
1.012	i
1.013	j
1.014	a
1.015	b
1.016	l
1.017	h
1.018	e
1.019	d
1.020	f
1.021	k
1.022	Mesopotamia
1.023	Sumerians
1.024	Adam
1.025	God
1.026	the sun's radiation
1.027	strata
1.028	petroleum
1.029	g
1.030	h
1.031	e
1.032	c
1.033	b
1.034	a
1.035	i
1.036	j
1.037	f
1.038	d
1.039	l

1.040-1.042 Examples:

1.040 Oil and coal were formed from dead animals and plants over a period of years.

1.041 The land was everywhere the same; the climate was like a hothouse: warm and humid. The soil was rich.

1.042 Mountain ranges and volcanoes appeared; chasms opened. Hills fell. Oceans washed beaches away.

SECTION 2

2.1	c
2.2	e
2.3	d
2.4	e
2.5	b
2.6	c
2.7	f
2.8	a
2.9	a
2.10	e
2.11	d
2.12	f
2.13	g *or* h
2.14	h
2.15	g *or* h
2.16	h
2.17	h
2.18	c
2.19	Mediterranean
2.20	Minoan

2.21 Either order:
   a. plumbing
   b. paintings

2.22 Mycenaean

2.23 a. Egyptians
    b. Phoenicians

2.24 Either order:
   a. history
   b. science

2.25 400s B.C.

2.26 Any order:
   a. Etruscans
   b. Greeks
   c. Egyptians

2.27 Any order:
   a. roads
   b. aqueducts
   c. coded laws
   or Latin

2.28	d
2.29	c
2.30	a
2.31	d
2.32	b
2.33	a
2.34	b
2.35	b
2.36	b

2.37 Any order:
   a. Ethiopia
   b. Bantus
   c. Hottentots
   d. Nubians
   e. Kongo
   or Lubas; Aksum; Ghana; Mali

2.38 Either order:
   a. They intermarried with them.
   b. They pushed them into the rainforest or desert to live.

2.39	a
2.40	b
2.41	c
2.42	c
2.43	a
2.44	b
2.45	b
2.46	a
2.47	c
2.48	false
2.49	true
2.50	true
2.51	true
2.52	false
2.53	true

2.54 Either order:
   a. Tyre
   b. Sidon

2.55 Either order:
   a. Carthaginians
   b. Greeks

2.56	compass
2.57	Leif Erickson
2.58	Robert Fulton
2.59	canals

2.60 Either order:
   a. Panama
   b. Suez

2.61 dredging

2.62 Either order:
   a. diesel
   b. nuclear (atomic)

2.63 Either order:
   a. oars
   b. sails

2.64	b
2.65	d
2.66	a
2.67	a
2.68	c
2.69	b
2.70	d

2.71 Example:
Open-pit mines could be filled and covered once mining is completed. The ground could be brought back to its original contours and planted with grass, trees, or crops.

2.72 a

2.73 c

2.74 b

2.75 Any order:
   a. availability of jobs
   b. access to religious and cultural activities
   c. breakdown of feudal system
   or looking for better way of life

2.76 Any order:
   a. United States
   b. Canada
   c. India

2.77 Any order:
   a. railroads
   b. canals
   c. by sea
   or by turnpike

2.78 Either order:
   a. dams
   b. aqueducts
   or irrigation

2.79 Teacher check

2.80 Either order:
   a. coal
   b. petroleum

2.81 sludge

2.82 Example:
the study of living organisms in relationship to their environment

2.83 Example:
dumping pollutants into the air and water to be carried away

2.84 Example:
It would mean the recycling of natural resources that would otherwise be wasted. Scarring of the land could be repaired. Water and air would not be poisoned as they are now.

SELF TEST 2

2.01 b

2.02 a

2.03 c

2.04 a

2.05 a

2.06 c

2.07 b

2.08 c

2.09 a

2.010 a

2.011 g

2.012 k

2.013 a

2.014 i

2.015 f

2.016 c

2.017 b

2.018 j

2.019 d

2.020 e

2.021 Either order:
   a. coal
   b. petroleum

2.022 nuclear

2.023 fossil

2.024 replenish
   or subdue

2.025 a. Ararat
   b. Turkey

2.026 Lydians

2.027 Assyrians

2.028 Hebrew

2.029 Chinese

2.030 Mayans

2.031 a. Andes
   b. South America

2.032 Aztec

2.033 Either order:
   a. compass
   b. astrolabe

2.034 Either order:
   a. Panama
   b. Suez

2.035 true

2.036 true

2.037 true

2.038 c

2.039 d

2.040 e

2.041 a

2.042 b

SECTION 3

3.1   b
3.2   a
3.3   c
3.4   c
3.5   Examples:
       a. Diplomacy is the art and practice of
           conducting negotiations between nations.
       b. Nations desiring to live in peace should
           use diplomacy in a spirit of tolerance and
           understanding of the point of view of
           others.
3.6   Example:
       The Antichrist will likely be a proud, vain
       deceiver. He will cause all men to live under
       his bondage to satisfy his greed for power.
       He will sacrifice anyone who stands in his
       way.
3.7   lamb
3.8   Jerusalem
3.9   rearranged
3.10 Either order:
       a. heavens
       b. firmament
3.11 Daniel
3.12 judge
3.13 peace
3.14 thousand
3.15 saints
3.16 God in heaven
3.17 Example:
       They shall not eat meat; "the lion shall eat
       straw like the ox."
3.18 Any order:
       a. tears
       b. death
       c. sorrow
       d. crying
       e. pain

SELF TEST 3

3.01   false
3.02   true
3.03   true
3.04   false
3.05   false
3.06   false
3.07   true
3.08   true
3.09   true
3.010 true
3.011 England
3.012 Babel
3.013 glacier
3.014 Either order:
        a. Panama
        b. Suez
3.015 open-pit
3.016 the flood
3.017 Armageddon
3.018 Antichrist
3.019 ten
3.020 League of Nations
3.021 Either order:
        a. coal
        b. petroleum
3.022 Middle East
3.023 conquering lamb
3.024 b
3.025 g
3.026 c
3.027 a
3.028 h
3.029 f
3.030 a
3.031 f
3.032 e
3.033 e
3.034 g
3.035 e
3.036 d
3.037 a
3.038 c
3.039-3.041 Examples:
3.039 Oil and coal were formed from dead animals
        and plants under the pressure of tons of
        rocks and mud over thousands of years.
3.040 The topography will be rearranged.
        Mountains and islands will be moved.
        Stars will fall into the oceans, killing marine
        life. Rivers will be poisoned.
3.041 Men will be with God and He with them.
        There will be no more tears, death, sorrow,
        crying or pain. Everything will be new.

LIFEPAC TEST

1.	b		**33.**	Antichrist
2.	c		**34.**	one
3.	a		**35.**	League of Nations
4.	c		**36.**	conquering lamb
5.	a		**37.**	rearranged
6.	b		**38.**	d
7.	d		**39.**	a
8.	a		**40.**	e
9.	b		**41.**	b
10.	c		**42.**	c

11. Example:
They used water craft or simple and primitive construction.

12. Example:
Ecology is the study of living organisms in relationship to their environment.

13. Example:
reusing refuse such as metal, glass, and paper to make new products

14. h
15. c
16. d
17. a
18. g
19. f
20. i
21. e
22. j
23. b
24. 2
25. 3
26. 5
27. 4
28. 1
29. 7
30. 6

31. Examples:
a. using sludge for fertilizer
b. using sewage for landfill
c. recycling glass and paper

32. Any order:
a. no more tears
b. no more death
c. no more sorrow
d. no more pain
e. no more crying

ALTERNATE LIFEPAC TEST

1. c
2. a
3. a
4. a
5. d
6. a
7: a
8. c
9. b
10. a
11. He dammed up rivers and created reservoirs to hold lakes of water. Then he built water filtering plants to clean up his water so that he could drink it. In some places he used canals to irrigate farms near his cities.
12. He built hydroelectric plants in the dams he built on rivers. He also built coal and oil-burning generators so that electricity could be provided for the cities.
13. He built modern highways, streets, and freeways as well as subways and railways to transport the people to and around in his cities.
14. d
15. a
16. f
17. j
18. c
19. b
20. g
21. i
22. e
23. h
24. gold
25. smog
26. sea
27. Italy
28. war
   or battle
29. hell
30. fire
31. New Jerusalem
32. Jesus Christ
33. geologists
34. c
35. b
36. a
37. a
38. c

HISTORY & GEOGRAPHY 906

ALTERNATE LIFEPAC TEST

NAME _____

DATE _____

SCORE _____

Write the letter for the correct answer on each line (each answer, 2 points).

1. The earth's first climate _____ .
   a. was very cold
   b. was harsh
   c. was spring-like
   d. had four seasons

2. The confusion of man's languages happened at _____ .
   a. Babel
   b. Memphis
   c. Phoenicia
   d. Kish

3. The Sumerians used wedge-shaped characters in their alphabet for writing in clay.
   This type of writing was called _____ .
   a. cuneiform
   b. hieroglyphic
   c. papyrus
   d. lettering

4. Before sinning, early man lived _____ .
   a. long lifespan
   b. in fear of dinosaurs
   c. in the trees
   d. as a proto man

5. A blend of two metals is known as _____ .
   a. open pit mining
   b. an outflow
   c. ductile
   d. an alloy

6. Mining was revived after the _____ .
   a. Dark Ages passed
   b. atomic age arrived
   c. tower of Babel fell
   d. Golden Age came

7. During the Industrial Revolution many cities in Europe were _____ .
   a. very dirty and crowded
   b. like paradise
   c. abandoned
   d. paved

8. Merchants from Europe expanded trade in the new world by selling their wares in _____ .
   a. Japan
   b. India
   c. their colonies in America
   d. Siberia

9. The waste that causes a buildup of sludge in river bottoms is called _____ .
   a. slag
   b. effluent
   c. smog
   d. alloy

10. The greatest source of air pollution is from _____ .
    a. generating electricity from coal
    b. hydroelectric generation of electricity
    c. dumping garbage at city dumps

Answer these questions (each answer, 5 points).

11. How did man develop nature's resources to provide for the water supply needed for a city?

    _____

    _____

    _____

    _____

    _____

12. How did man develop nature's resources to provide for the energy needs of a city?

    _____

    _____

    _____

    _____

    _____

13. How did man develop nature's resources to provide for the transportation needs of a city?

    _____

    _____

    _____

    _____

    _____

Match these items (each answer, 2 points).

14. _____ pestilence

15. _____ deluge

16. _____ millennium

17. _____ ecology

18. _____ refinery

19. _____ famine

20. _____ technology

21. _____ Antichrist

22. _____ clipper

23. _____ marsh

a. Noah's Flood

b. a drought

c. raw materials become merchandise

d. a plague of insects

e. a sailing ship

f. one thousand years

g. development of better engineering skills

h. a swampy area

i. mark of the beast

j. a good balance in nature

Complete these sentences (each answer, 3 points).

24. The metal that is more ductile than other metals is _____ .

25. Dirty air is called _____ .

26. The Mediterranean is the name of a(n) _____ .

27. Rome is a great city in the country of _____ .

28. Armageddon will be a place of _____ .

29. The wicked shall be judged and sent to _____ .

30. The present earth will be destroyed by _____ .

31. The city that will come down out of heaven will be _____ .

32. The ruler during the millennium will be _____ .

33. Those who study the earth's topography are called _____ .

Write the letter for the correct answer on each line (each answer, 2 points).

34. Jesus Christ is called _____ .
    a. the king of Babylon
    b. a warmonger
    c. the Prince of Peace

35. Charles Darwin was _____ .
    a. a Creationist
    b. an evolutionist
    c. a prophet

36. Daniel Jackling advanced the idea of _____ .
    a. open pit mining
    b. the theory of evolution
    c. city planning

37. Around A.D. 1000 the Vikings were great explorers. They were from _____ .
    a. Norway and Denmark
    b. Russia
    c. Phoenicia

38. The people who established city-states along the Tigris and Euphrates rivers
    were the _____ .
    a. Greeks
    b. Egyptians
    c. Sumerians

HISTORY & GEOGRAPHY 907

Unit 7: Regions of the World

TEACHER NOTES

MATERIALS NEEDED FOR LIFEPAC	
Required	Suggested
None	• Bible encyclopedia • reference books or online sources

ADDITIONAL LEARNING ACTIVITIES

Section 1: Region — A Definition

1. Using a globe, point out to students the equator, the prime meridian, the continents, and the various regions studied in the section.

2. If you have lived in another region of the world or have visited another region, explain the differences in climate, geography, social customs, and politics that existed there. Invite students to contribute to the discussion if applicable.

3. Together, make a relief map of the world (if the class is large) or one of a continent with which your class is relatively unfamiliar.

4. Invite a meteorologist to speak to the class about climatic differences in North America or in the world.

5. Have students research one of the Judeo-Christian religions (make sure students are researching different religions). Have students share new information with each other.

6. Help students arrange an interview with a person who has lived in another region of the world. They should have questions prepared in advance. Then, have students share with the class how that person's life in another region differs from life in your own region.

Section 2: World Regional Patterns — A Survey

1. As a class, make a climate chart that lists the climatic regions and the conditions that prevail in each region.

2. Explain to students and conduct a class discussion on the interrelationships of the major regions discussed in the section.

3. Assign a group research and discussion project on prejudice with these directions: Be specific. Study one group of people and how prejudice affected their treatment of another people. Choose any time or place in history.

4. Show a film or video about another region or continent. Afterward, discuss the film as a class, focusing on the differences and similarities between the film subject and your own region.

5. Have students research and report on an unfamiliar religion in another country.

6. Have the class draw a map of the world and label the regions they have studied in this section.

Section 3: Europe — Political and Economic Regions

1. Have the class explain how the major common markets work.

2. As a class, contrast the common markets, free trade associations, and the stock market and trade policies of the United States.

3. Invite an economist to speak to the class about the common markets and free trade associations. Have the class prepare questions in advance.

4. If possible, arrange a visit to a stock exchange to see how the United States stock market works. Or, have students view pictures and information online.

5. Have students research an economic problem that one of the economic divisions in the world is presently facing.

6. Have students research the United States trade policy and compare it to that of the European Free Trade Association or the European Union.

7. Assign students to research and report on the economic problems in one of the former communist countries.

Administer the LIFEPAC Test

The test is to be administered in one session. Give no help except with directions.
Evaluate the tests and review areas where the students have done poorly.
Review the pages and activities that stress the concepts tested.
If necessary, administer the Alternate LIFEPAC Test.

ANSWER KEYS

SECTION 1

1.1	physical
1.2	Gospel
1.3	characteristic
1.4	significant effect
1.5	isolate
1.6	They are physical barriers.
1.7	They are the Northern Hemisphere, Southern Hemisphere, Eastern Hemisphere, and Western Hemisphere.
1.8	They are Europe-Asia-Africa, North America-South America, Australia, and Antarctica.
1.9	They are Europe, Asia, Africa, North America, South America, Australia, and Antarctica.
1.10	It was similar to that inside a greenhouse.
1.11	The tropics, the middle latitudes, the polar regions, and deserts will be covered.
1.12	census
1.13	skeletal
1.14	Nationalism
1.15	Any order:
	a. Judeo-Christian
	b. Islam
	c. Eastern religions
	d. animism
	e. secular ideologies
1.16	the Cold War
1.17	free trade zones *or* economic spheres
1.18	Free World Bloc, Communist Bloc, Third World Bloc
1.19	superficial
1.20	false
1.21	true
1.22	true
1.23	false

SELF TEST 1

1.01	c
1.02	d
1.03	b
1.04	a
1.05	prime meridian
1.06	attitudes
1.07	continents
1.08	Gospel
1.09	A region is an area in which a certain characteristic is dominant.
1.010	It is worth studying if it has a significant effect on a majority of the population
1.011	Any order:
	a. Northern Hemisphere
	b. Southern Hemisphere
	c. Eastern Hemisphere
	d. Western Hemisphere
1.012	Any four: politics, economics, religion, geography, climate, race
1.013	b
1.014	a
1.015	a
1.016	c
1.017	b

SECTION 2

2.1 Any order:
   a. Arctic Ocean
   b. Atlantic Ocean
   c. Ural Mountains
   or Asia
   d. Mediterranean Sea

2.2 Either order:
   a. Sweden
   b. Norway

2.3 Either order:
   a. Denmark
   b. Finland

2.4 British Isles

2.5 Either order:
   a. Spain
   b. Portugal

2.6 Any order:
   a. Italy
   b. Greece
   c. Albania
   d. Macedonia

2.7 Ural Mountains

2.8 true

2.9 false

2.10 false

2.11 c

2.12 c

2.13 a

2.14 c

2.15 f

2.16 g

2.17 a

2.18 d

2.19 b

2.20 e

2.21 h

2.22 false

2.23 true

2.24 true

2.25 Either order:
   a. Atlantic
   b. Pacific

2.26 Any order:
   a. Canada
   b. Greenland
   c. United States
   d. Mexico

2.27 Either order:
   a. Alaska
   b. Hawaii

2.28 Mexico

2.29 the west coast

2.30 c

2.31 a

2.32 b

2.33 b

2.34 b

2.35 a

2.36 true

2.37 false

2.38 false

2.39 Mediterranean

2.40 Sahara Desert

2.41 Madagascar

2.42 climate

2.43 equator

2.44 tropics

2.45 a. jungle
   b. rainforest
   c. savanna
   d. deserts

2.46 four

2.47 steppes

2.48 50°F

2.49 Any order:
   a. South America
   b. Australia
   c. Africa

2.50 Europe

2.51 middle latitudes

2.52 b

2.53 a

2.54 h

2.55 f

2.56 c

2.57 d

2.58 g

2.59 Racial prejudice comes from pride thinking we are better than other people, and lack of trust in God.

2.60 John 3:16 says that God loved the world, all kinds of people, and whoever believes is saved and is a brother in Christ.

2.61 true

2.62 false

2.63 individualism or respect for the individual

2.64 to subdue the earth and have dominion over it

2.65 as honoring the Lord

2.66 "Waste not, want not."

2.67 devotion to God

2.68 God's Word

2.69 b

2.70 a

2.71 a

2.72 c

2.73 Any order:
a. Believe in one God, Allah, and Muhammad, his prophet
b. Prayers 5 times a day
c. Fasting during Ramadan
d. Poor tax
e. Pilgrimage to Mecca

2.74 Jesus was a prophet. Christians are "people of the book."

2.75 Most of the Near East, Pakistan, much of India, north Africa, Spain, and southern France.

2.76 Either order:
a. caliphs
b. imams

2.77 c

2.78 d

2.79 a

2.80 b

2.81 Any order:
a. Hinduism
b. Buddhism
c. Shintoism

2.82 pantheistic

2.83 polytheistic

2.84 animals

2.85 Either order:
a. Middle Way
b. Noble Eightfold Path

2.86 Karma

2.87 Buddhism

2.88 Gautama Buddha

2.89 suffering

2.90 Nirvana

2.91 b

2.92 a

2.93 b

2.94 b

2.95 a

2.96 The belief that lifeless objects have spirits.

2.97 The investment of lifeless objects with spirits and using those objects as good luck charms.

2.98 Seeking to please deities by vile rites and trances.

2.99 There is no loving God to whom he can appeal, only spirits he must placate.

2.100 Either order:
a. control man
b. save man

2.101 atheism

2.102 God

2.103 private property

2.104 utopian

2.105 a. proletariat
b. capitalists

2.106 everything

2.107 brute force

2.108 capitalist

2.109 collapsed

2.110 idolized

2.111 Christians

2.112 humanism

2.113 a. creation
b. divine control of history

2.114 evolution

2.115 progress in the form of technology, wealth, education, and personal comfort

2.116 They leave out devotion to God.

2.117 Experiences which will reveal reality to them.

2.118 drugs, alcohol, Eastern religions, political extremism, and suicide

2.119 Teacher check

SELF TEST 2

2.01 false
2.02 true
2.03 true
2.04 true
2.05 false
2.06 false
2.07 true
2.08 true
2.09 true
2.010 false
2.011 Islam
2.012 Indian Subcontinent
2.013 suffering
2.014 Gospel
2.015 God's Word
or the Bible
2.016 reincarnation
2.017 fear
2.018 polar
2.019 Judeo-Christian
2.020 Muhammad

SECTION 3

3.1 Cold War
3.2 a. Free World
b. Communist
c. Third World
3.3 satellites
3.4 common enemy
3.5 Mikhail Gorbachev
3.6 Hungary and Czechoslovakia
3.7 collapse
3.8 Third World
3.9 false
3.10 false
3.11 true
3.12 true
3.13 false
3.14 true
3.15 true
3.16 false
3.17 The Third World was able to obtain weapons, money, and technology from either side during the Cold War.
3.18 The people had no incentive to work hard. Thus, production was low and of poor quality. The cost of supplying weapons to terrorists and support for communist governments world-wide overwhelmed the economy.
3.19 To combat communism. When communism fell, so did the three-bloc system.
3.20 Any three:
a. Bosnia-Herzegovina
b. Croatia
c. Armenia
or Azerbaijan; Russia; Georgia
3.21 Teacher check
3.22 economic prosperity and a United States of Europe
3.23 A common market in coal, steel, iron, and scrap metal.
3.24 Jean Monnet
3.25 Any order:
a. Belgium
b. France
c. Italy
d. Luxembourg
e. the Netherlands
f. West Germany
3.26 to live, work, and vote
3.27 European Parliament
3.28 Court of Justice
3.29 Commission
3.30 Council of Ministers

3.31	f
3.32	b
3.33	d
3.34	a
3.35	c
3.36	To counter the formation of the European Community.
3.37	The EFTA is less comprehensive than the European Union. It does not regulate anything except trade between its members.
3.38	a. EFTA Council
	b. one representative from each member state
3.39	none
3.40	Any order:
	a. United States
	b. Canada
	c. Mexico
3.41	To eliminate tariffs on most goods moving between the countries over a ten-year period.
3.42	no
3.43	1967
3.44	Gradually remove all tariffs among themselves
3.45	a. economic
	b. cultural
	c. social
3.46	General Agreement on Tariffs and Trade
3.47	120
3.48	transparency and non-discrimination
3.49	economic regions

SELF TEST 3

3.01	g
3.02	i
3.03	h
3.04	d
3.05	a
3.06	f
3.07	c
3.08	j
3.09	e
3.010	b
3.011	economic
3.012	collapse
3.013	Third World
3.014	utopia
3.015	trade
3.016	tariffs
3.017	European Union
3.018	Mikhail Gorbachev
3.019	Monnet
3.020	European Coal and Steel Community
3.021	For fear of mutual destruction or destruction of the world.
3.022	EFTA covers only trade between the members; European Union covers much more.
3.023	a. United States
	b. Canada
	c. Mexico
3.024	Association of Southeast Asian Nations
3.025	to live, work, and vote
3.026	false
3.027	false
3.028	true
3.029	true
3.030	true

LIFEPAC TEST

1. c
2. d
3. b
4. a
5. c
6. a
7. b
8. c
9. c
10. a
11. e
12. a
13. d
14. c
15. b
16. true
17. false
18. true
19. false
20. false
21. true
22. true
23. true
24. false
25. false
26. region
27. greenhouse
28. Europe
29. Asia
30. Central America
31. individual
32. Koran
33. Ural Mountains
34. secular
35. European Union

ALTERNATE LIFEPAC TEST

1. g
2. a
3. c
4. j
5. h
6. i
7. e
8. b
9. f
10. d
11. false
12. true
13. false
14. true
15. false
16. false
17. false
18. true
19. false
20. false
21. b
22. c
23. d
24. a
25. b
26. c
27. a
28. c
29. c
30. b
31. Antarctica
32. Any order:
    a. Free World (West)
    b. the Communist World (East)
    c. the Third World (neutral or unaligned nations)
33. utopia
34. desert
35. Sahara
36. Brahmans
37. Russia
38. Jean Monnet
39. Islam
40. Any order:
    a. U.S.
    b. Canada
    c. Mexico

HISTORY & GEOGRAPHY 907

ALTERNATE LIFEPAC TEST

NAME _____

DATE _____

SCORE _____

82

102

Match these items (each answer, 2 points).

1. _____ equator
2. _____ prime meridian
3. _____ region
4. _____ tropics
5. _____ polar regions
6. _____ European
7. _____ Hinduism
8. _____ communism
9. _____ European Free Trade Association
10. _____ European Union

a. divides Eastern and Western hemispheres

b. collapsed in Europe in 1991

c. area where certain characteristics are common to the people who live there

d. building a united Europe

e. religion of India

f. eliminated most tariffs among its members

g. divides the Northern Hemisphere from the Southern Hemisphere

h. farthest from equator

i. Europe, Middle East, North Africa

j. climatic region close to the equator

Answer *true* **or** *false* (each answer, 2 points).

11. _____ Mikhail Gorbachev made communist Russia a great power after World War II.

12. _____ The period from the end of World War II until 1991 was the Cold War.

13. _____ The three traditional races were based on blood analysis.

14. _____ Great Britain is an island containing the countries of England, Scotland, and Wales.

15. _____ Europe is the largest continent.

16. _____ The Panama Canal divides the continents of North America and Central America.

17. _____ The largest country in South America is Venezuela.

18. _____ The culture of Islam was begun by an Arab named Muhammad.

19. _____ Eastern religions usually involve animal sacrifice.

20. _____ Common markets have largely disappeared because they became ineffective.

Write the letter for the correct answer on each line (each answer, 2 points).

21. Which of these is an example of the relationship between geography and climate? _____
    a. People migrating away from the equator.
    b. People in the mountains of Arizona wearing heavy wool (warm) clothing.
    c. People in China being communists.
    d. People in parts of Canada being French Catholic.

22. The climatic region located about halfway between the equator and the poles is

    called the _____.
    a. desert   b. grasslands
    c. middle latitudes   d. tropical region

23. The largest continent is _____ .
    a. North America   b. Australia
    c. Europe   d. Asia

24. Australia is located _____ .
    a. where the Indian and Pacific oceans meet
    b. between the Mediterranean Sea and the Persian Gulf
    c. in the Atlantic Ocean between Bermuda and Europe

25. The ideals of the Judeo-Christian culture are based upon _____ .
    a. the teachings of Moses   b. God's Word
    c. theological interpretations   d. spiritual experience

26. In the Muslim religion, Muhammad is regarded as _____ .
    a. a god   b. a saint
    c. a prophet   d. a human

27. In the Hindu religion, *karma* refers to _____ .
    a. reincarnation   b. death
    c. the religion's sacred book   d. daily prayer

28. Buddhism teaches that _____ .
    a. polygamy is permitted   b. animals have souls
    c. all of life is a form of suffering   d. no one can truly comprehend Buddha

29. The eastern religion that teaches extreme patriotism, family loyalty, and ancestor worship
    is _____ .
    a. Hinduism   b. Buddhism
    c. Shintoism   d. a, b, and c

30. The most powerful branch of the European Union's governmental structure is _____ .
    a. Representative Council   b. Court of Justice
    c. Council of Ministers   d. executive branch

Complete these sentences (each answer, 3 points).

31. The least inhabited continent is _____ .

32. The three principal political divisions in the world during the Cold War were

    a. _____ ,

    b. _____ , and

    c. _____ .

33. Communism promised to create a(n) _____ on earth.

34. The driest climatic region is the _____ .

35. Most of the countries in Africa overlap the _____ Desert.

36. In the Hindu religion, priests are called _____ .

37. The largest country in Asia is _____ .

38. The principal promoter of European economic unity was the French statesman

    _____ .

39. The Koran is the holy book of _____ .

40. a. _____ , b. _____ , and

    c. _____ were part of NAFTA.

HISTORY & GEOGRAPHY 908

Unit 8: Man and His Environment

TEACHER NOTES

MATERIALS NEEDED FOR LIFEPAC	
Required	Suggested
None	• Bible encyclopedia • reference books or online sources

ADDITIONAL LEARNING ACTIVITIES

Section 1: Man and His Physical Environment

1. As a class, conduct an experiment to show how wastes pollute the water. Such experiments can be found in Science textbooks or online.

2. Discuss with students their specific bad health habits and how they believe they could be improved.

3. Invite a former drug addict to speak to your class about drug addiction, its consequences, and its treatment. Local drug treatment agencies often provide such speakers. Also look into "Teen Challenge."

4. Arrange to visit a forester or ask a forester to speak to your class. Ask them to explain ways of preserving the forests, how forest fires are prevented and put out when they occur, and how citizens can make the forester's job easier.

5. Arrange for students to interview a nutritionist about the effects of not eating a balanced diet. Most foods are healthy if consumed in moderation. Students should ask about the harmful effects on the body if one eats too much of a certain food item, which foods are healthier than others, and what effects eating disorders (anorexia, bulimia, overeating) have on growing and developing bodies. Have students share information.

6. Have the class keep a log of the air quality in your community for one month. What factors affect the air quality on any given day? What ways might citizens help to improve the air quality? Discuss in class.

Section 2: Man and His Social Environment

1. Discuss in detail the free enterprise system of economics. Use charts and other visual aids to clarify the explanation.

2. Gather pamphlets, articles, and other information on careers, and have the information available in the classroom for students to read.

3. Invite a career counselor to speak to your class about careers and family life. Ask the person to be available after the speech to answer specific student questions.

4. Arrange a visit to a local industry. Ask the person who takes you on a tour of the factory to explain and show examples of the governmental regulations with which that industry must comply. Ask to see examples of forms that must be completed and sent to various bureaus.

5. Provide the following directions: Investigate a career that you might be interested in pursuing when you become an adult. Find out what education or training you will need, what kinds of duties you will be performing, where you are likely to be working, the salary you can expect, and hazards connected with the career. Investigate also the impact your choice of career will have on your lifestyle.

6. Instruct students to learn all they can about one of the federal programs now in operation in this country. Assign an oral report to the class.

Section 3: Man and His Responsibilities to His Environment

1. Lead students in thinking of ways they can conserve resources and energy in their own school building. List the ways on a chart and encourage students to practice them daily. At the end of a month, discuss any improvements.

2. Help students to practice Biblical and Christian principles in their personal dealings and dealings with other students and adults in the school. Have students keep a log of problems they have had and how they solved them through the application of Christian and Biblical principles.

3. Conduct a recycling campaign in your school. Then, arrange to visit a recycling plant for students to see what happens to the items. If you receive money for your donated items, use the money to buy an item for your school or donate it to a worthy charity.

4. Invite a clergyman or counselor who practices biblical principles to speak to your class on the causes, results, and cures for stress. Find out the measures you can take to avoid stress.

5. Have students visit the website of the Sierra Club or other ecological organization: Look at the projects that the organization is working on. Do you agree or disagree with the philosophy, purposes, and goals of the organization? How does the philosophy of the organization support or contradict what is taught in scripture? Construct a chart that compares what the organization believes to what is given in scripture.

6. Assign students to write a paper on how you can have a fulfilling adult life through the practice of biblical and Christian principles.

Administer the LIFEPAC Test

The test is to be administered in one session. Give no help except with directions.
Evaluate the tests and review areas where the students have done poorly.
Review the pages and activities that stress the concepts tested.
If necessary, administer the Alternate LIFEPAC Test.

ANSWER KEYS

SECTION 1

1.1   a. ecology
        b. ecologist

1.2   Any order:
        a. high cost of farming
            or low profits
        b. increasing taxes
            or increased cost of living
        c. offers of large payments for their acreage
            or population growth

1.3   Example:
        farmers name

1.4   URLs from organizations like the following should be listed:
        – U.S. Department of Agriculture
        – Cooperative Extension Service
        – County Agricultural Agent
        – State University Agricultural Department

1.5   true

1.6   true

1.7   false

1.8   true

1.9   true

1.10 coal

1.11 Any order:
        a. sulfur compounds
        b. carbon monoxide
        c. hydrogen
        d. nitrogen dioxide

1.12 energy

1.13 Any order:
        a. air pollution
            or food additives
        b. noise
            or auto accidents
        c. water pollution
            or garbage contamination
        d. poisons in our food chain
            or exposure to colds or flu

1.14 true

1.15 false

1.16 false

1.17 Any order:
        a. headaches
        b. rapid heartbeat
        c. guilt
        d. peptic ulcers
        e. weakness
        f. loss of appetite
        or inability to sleep; excitement; fright; irritation; laughter; high blood pressure

1.18 f

1.19 e

1.20 a

1.21 h

1.22 g

1.23 c

1.24 d

1.25 environment

1.26 temple

1.27 smokers

1.28 psychological

1.29 sensitivities

1.30 Hint:
        Your interview should have included the reason some young people start smoking, how it affects the smoker's health, and how hard it is to stop.

1.31 true

1.32 false

1.33 true

1.34 true

1.35 true

1.36 false

1.37 derivatives

1.38 withdrawal

1.39 wars

1.40 moods

1.41 Teacher check

1.42 Examples:
        a. sugar, corn, wheat *or* oat flour
        b. sugar and dextrose, enriched (bleached) flour, instant pudding
        c. sugar, corn syrup, artificial flavor and food coloring
        d. corn
        e. carbonated water, sugar, citric acid

1.43   the United States
1.44   pollutants
1.45   1918
1.46   National Environmental Policy Act
1.47   wilderness
1.48   watershed
1.49   floods
1.50   Teacher check
1.51   Examples:
    a. lights
    b. tooth brush if electric
    c. toaster
    d. oven, stove, *or* microwave
    e. refrigerator
    f. juicer if electric
    g. electric clock *or* radio
    h. telephone
    i. radio if turned on
    j. dishwasher
    k. washing machine
    l. dryer
    m. hair dryer
    n. hot water heater
    o. auto *or* bus
    p. heating *or* cooling
1.52   the requirements of the Environmental Protection Agency that the land be returned to its prior quality
1.53   Petroleum engineers.
As national priorities, space exploration and scientific space research have been surpassed by the need to become independent of imported oil. Only twenty years of liquid oil are left.
Nuclear power plants take too long to build, but environmentalists are slowing some projects even further. Oil engineers have special training in discovery and refinement of oil and gas.
1.54   You should have sensed God's mighty power in the creation of all the earth and all living things. The natural environment is not an accident but a planned creation that we should love and respect.
1.55   true
1.56   true
1.57   false
1.58   true
1.59   Any order:
    a. production of wood products
    b. maintenance of watersheds
    c. recreation
    d. habitat for wildlife
    or air quality

SELF TEST 1

1.01   d
1.02   c
1.03   f
1.04   e
1.05   b
1.06   a
1.07   g
1.08   h
1.09 -1.013 Any order; suggested answers:
1.09   cities grow and take over farmland
1.010 water and/or air pollution increases
1.011 new jobs must be found by families or both parents must work
1.012 adjustments must be made in individual and family life styles
1.013 marriages are put under stress *or* welfare increases
1.014 shale
1.015 Any order:
    a. hydrogen
    b. sulphur compounds
    c. carbon monoxide
    d. nitrogen dioxide
1.016 psychosomatic illnesses
1.017 carcinogen
1.018 sugar
1.019 dental cavities *or* obesity
1.020 fossil fuels
1.021 increases
1.022 decrease
1.023 increase
1.024 decreased
1.025 increase
1.026 increase
1.027 increase
1.028 b
1.029 c
1.030 a
1.031 c
1.032 c
1.033 a
1.034 d
1.035 b
1.036 d
1.037 c
1.038 Hint:
Your answer should indicate the delicate balance of nature or at least the interdependence of plant and animal life. You should give some indication that damage can be done to nature by interfering with food chains.

1.039	true
1.040	true
1.041	true
1.042	true
1.043	false
1.044	true
1.045	true
1.046	true
1.047	true
1.048	true

SECTION 2

2.1 Social Security

2.2 Great Society

2.3 assure a continuing income

2.4 gave money to unmarried mothers to pay for food and clothing of their children

2.5 provided for vocational training so they could be self-supporting

2.6 Welfare State

2.7 Any order:
   a. New Deal of 1930s
   b. Great Society of 1960s
   c. attempt to reform the whole system in 1970s

2.8 1960s

2.9 Cities and states cannot afford to keep up with rapidly increasing costs.

2.10 Any order:
   a. Department of Housing and Urban Development (HUD)
   b. Department of Transportation
   c. Office of Economic Opportunity (OEO)

2.11 Proposition 13

2.12 Occupation Safety and Health Act (OSHA)

2.13 free enterprise

2.14 Office of Economic Opportunity

2.15 federal minimum wage

2.16 Affirmative Action

2.17 United States Department of Labor

2.18 Any order:
   a. practical nurses
   b. computer programmers
   c. technicians

2.19 Any order:
   a. a
   b. c
   c. f

2.20 kindergarten

2.21 Hint:
   Your answer should describe a planned approach to the world of work.
   Select an area of enjoyable work—
   not a single dead-end job or jobs.

2.22 Teacher check

2.23 Teacher check

2.24 Teacher check

2.25 Any order:

    a. motivation and values

    b. higher education levels of women promote longer working

    c. divorces leave little money for the wife to live on

    d. economics; increasing living costs *or* changing values

2.26 50 percent

2.27 More women will continue to work because the causes of their need to work will increase.

2.28 a. $8.30

    b. $1,425.50

2.29 a. $77.23

    b. $78.80

    c. $63.51

SELF TEST 2

2.01 b

2.02 c

2.03 a

2.04 c

2.05 false

2.06 false

2.07 true

2.08 false

2.09 false

2.010 false

2.011 true

2.012 false

2.013 true

2.014 true

2.015 c

2.016 d

2.017 f

2.018 e

2.019 a

2.020 g

2.021 b

2.022 f

2.023 c

2.024 c

2.025 e

2.026 a

2.027 d

2.028 b

2.029 a

2.030 b

2.031 actual tuition, fees, living expenses, and loss of income while in school

2.032 jobs hard to get/competition high

2.033 good opportunities to get jobs in their field

2.034 pressures caused by financial strains

2.035 school and work

2.036 b

2.037 a

2.038 b

2.039 c

2.040 a

2.041 d

2.042 e

2.043 k

2.044 f

2.045 a

2.046 i, g

2.047 c

2.048 h, e

2.049 j

2.050 b

SECTION 3

3.1   Teacher check

3.2   Teacher check

3.3   Teacher check

3.4   Any order:
   a. putting trash in containers
   b. keeping noise down
   c. buying low phosphate soap and/or biodegradable products.

3.5   supporting an ecological group

3.6   Much more water is being used today than ever before.

3.7
   a. agriculture
   b. industry and electric utilities
   c. industry and electric utilities

3.8   industry and electric utilities

3.9   More people live here to use water. Also, each person uses more water today than in past years. Population increases mean increases in water use.

3.10   Hint:
   a. turn off lights, adjust the thermostat, replace old appliances with ones that are energy efficient
   b. collecting cans, paper, glass for recycling, and buying soda pop in returnable, not disposable, bottles
   c. car pool, walk or use a bike for short distances, go to the store less often

3.11   4 p.m. and 8 p.m.

3.12   Any order:
   a. truth
   b. honesty
   c. justice
   d. purity
   e. lovely things
   f. things of good report
   g. virtuousness
   h. praise

3.13   a
   d
   g
   h
   j
   k
   m
   n
   o

3.14   Teacher check

3.15   "For godly sorrow worketh repentance to salvation not to be repented of; but the sorrow of the world worketh death."
   a. repentance and salvation
   b. death

3.16   Teacher check

3.17   Teacher check

3.18   God

3.19   aptitude test/vocational test

3.20   Any order:
   a. the skill level needed to do the job
   b. union wage structures
   c. the amount of danger
   or distastefulness for the job

3.21   Hint:
   The answer should include an element of decision for a career and a calling or summons into that occupation by God.

3.22   Hint:
   The answer should reflect the fact that though man may have an idea to either say or do, the Lord actually gives the directions. Also, Solomon says that if the ways of a man pleases the Lord, that even his enemies will be at peace with him. Finally, Verse 8 says that righteousness is better than great money accompanied by unrighteousness.

3.23   family

3.24   discipline

3.25   true

3.26   false

3.27   true

SELF TEST 3

3.01   a
3.02   b
3.03-3.07 Examples:
3.03   pollute water with sewage
3.04   put phosphates in water
3.05   pour industrial waste in water
3.06   throw rubbish in streams and lakes
3.07   heat up water to where it kills fish
         or dump poison and non-biodegradable
         materials in sewers
3.08-3.012 Examples:
3.08   internal combustion engines
3.09   burn coal or garbage
3.010 industrial burning wastes
3.011 kill plant life that is needed to purify the air
3.012 smoke cigarettes
3.013-3.016 Examples:
3.013 write letters to Congress and federal agencies
3.014 support clubs, foundations, and research
         groups who publish information
3.015 vote
3.016 arrange for news broadcasts and political
         activity to bring out problem areas for public
         reaction
3.017-3.021 Examples:
3.017 smoking
3.018 living with too much stress, guilt, or worry
3.019 overuse of legal and illegal drugs
3.020 eating too much sugar-loaded food
3.021 too little recreation or exercise or not
         enough rest, maintaining bad feelings
         against other people, lead too busy a life,
         and so on
3.022 a, d, e, f, g, h
3.023 a, b, c,
3.024 b, c, i
3.025 true
3.026 true
3.027 false
3.028 true
3.029 false
3.030 false
3.031 true
3.032 true
3.033 true
3.034 false

3.035 church
3.036 talents
3.037 vocational testing/career planning
3.038 stress
3.039 carcinogen
3.040 the Great Society
3.041 OSHA
3.042 free enterprise
3.043 OPEC
3.044 taxpayer

LIFEPAC TEST

1.	j	**45.**	true
2.	e	**46.**	true
3.	g	**47.**	false
4.	l	**48.**	true
5.	b	**49.**	false
6.	k	**50.**	true
7.	f	**51.**	false
8.	d	**52.**	true
9.	a	**53.**	false
10.	c	**54.**	true
11.	i		
12.	h		
13.	a		
14.	c		
15.	b		
16.	c		
17.	a		
18.	c		
19.	b		
20.	a		
21.	c		
22.	b		
23.	b		
24.	a		
25.	c		
26.	b		
27.	true		
28.	false		
29.	false		
30.	false		
31.	false		
32.	false		
33.	false		
34.	true		
35.	Great Society		
36.	sins		

37. Either order:
a. physical
b. mental

38. Any order:
a. aptitudes
b. talents
c. interests

39. Jesus
40. discipline
or guide
41. church
42. megalopolis
43. hydroponic
44. phosphates

ALTERNATE LIFEPAC TEST

1.   d
2.   n
3.   a
4.   b
5.   j
6.   e
7.   c
8.   f
9.   i
10. g
11. true
12. true
13. false
14. false
15. true
16. true
17. false
18. false
19. true
20. true
21. c
22. b
23. a
24. d
25. c
26. c
27. b
28. a
29. d
30. d
31. nicotine
32. Any order:
    a. how to please God by pursuing
       the talents He has given you
    b. lifestyle
    c. whether you are people-oriented or
       fact oriented
    d. salary
33. Any three, any order:
    a. motivation
    b. more education/opportunities
    c. divorce
    or changes in our value structure,
       economics, independence

HISTORY & GEOGRAPHY 908

ALTERNATE LIFEPAC TEST

NAME _____

DATE _____

SCORE _____

72

90

Match these items (each answer, 2 points).

1. _____ Franklin Roosevelt
2. _____ Lyndon Johnson
3. _____ Sidney P. Marland, Jr.
4. _____ Eli Ginzberg
5. _____ Sierra Club
6. _____ OPEC
7. _____ OSHA
8. _____ AFDC
9. _____ Drs. Hammond and Horn
10. _____ Environmental Protection Agency

a. career education

b. explained reasons for women in the workforce

c. monitors safety in the work place

d. programs to solve economic problems in the 1930s

e. group of Arab oil-producing nations

f. free vocational counseling and job training for mothers

g. enforce regulations to help people interact with the environment

h. Great Society

i. sampled men's smoking habits

j. environmental lobbying group

Answer *true* **or** *false* (each answer, 2 points).

11. _____ Stress is the body's reaction to circumstances around it.

12. _____ God cautions people to live a moderate life in all ways.

13. _____ No organization in America today is absolutely committed to establishing, maintaining, and bettering family life.

14. _____ Most jobs in this country require a four-year college degree.

15. _____ In the year 2000, 85 percent of the population were living in cities.

16. _____ In the past, cities and industries dumped their wastes into the closest river, stream, or lake.

17. _____ Young people who grow up in families where the parents smoke are less likely to start smoking.

18. _____ After the passage of the Harrison Act in 1914, smaller percentages of people became addicted to opium, morphine, and heroin.

19. _____ Businesses over a certain size must pay a federal minimum wage.

20. _____ Efforts are made by the government to protect equality and opportunities.

Write the letter for the correct answer on each line (each answer, 2 points).

21. The primary reason that the cost of living has accelerated is _____ .
    a. people are buying on credit more items than they can afford
    b. workers are demanding higher wages
    c. higher housing and food costs
    d. interest rates have risen sharply

22. The average cost of a new home in January, 1979 was _____ .
    a. $35,000   b. $71,000   c. $25,000   d. $95,000

23. Programs to assist women, minorities, and people with disablities in finding employment are

    _____ .
    a. Affirmative Action programs
    b. Work Incentive programs
    c. Office of Economic Opportunity programs
    d. Department of Housing and Urban Development programs

24. People who retired under Social Security receive medical benefits through _____ .
    a. Medicaid
    b. Supplemental Security Income Program
    c. AFDC
    d. Medicare

25. The burning of coal has been curtailed in recent years because _____ .
    a. the nation's coal supply is low
    b. coal is very expensive to mine
    c. burning coal results in hazardous air pollution
    d. many people have been injured or killed while mining coal

26. An area of land that is drained by a stream is called _____ .
    a. a river bed   b. an oasis
    c. a watershed   d. a dam

27. Besides supplying lumber products, forests also provide _____ .
    a. possibilities for mining   b. better air quality
    c. fire shields   d. precious metals

28. High sugar levels in the blood were believed to have caused some children to become

    _____ .
    a. hyperactive   b. hypoglycemic
    c. hypochondriacs   d. depressed

29. Soaps that contained high levels of _____ had caused some lakes and rivers to become
    choked with fast-growing weeds and other plant life.
    a. bleach   b. lime
    c. lye   d. phosphates

30. Farms known as _____ farms enable crops fed certain minerals to be grown on shelves
    with no soil.
    a. natural   b. diversified
    c. dechemicalized   d. hydroponic

Complete these statements (each answer, 3 points).

31. People who smoke cigarettes eventually become addicted to a substance in the cigarettes

    called _____ .

32. In planning your life's work you should consider

    a. _____ ,

    b. _____ ,

    c. _____ and ,

    d. _____ .

33. Women are entering the workforce in great numbers because of

a. _____ ,

b. _____ and

c. _____ .

HISTORY & GEOGRAPHY 909

Unit 9: Tools of the Geographer

TEACHER NOTES

MATERIALS NEEDED FOR LIFEPAC	
Required	Suggested
None	• Bible • globe • maps of the world • stapler; transparent tape • salt; flour • black tape • sand or dirt • 9"x15" cake pan • cardboard–9"x12" • transparent plastic bags–approximately 10"x13" • water; tempera paints and brushes • mixing bowls • reference books or online sources

ADDITIONAL LEARNING ACTIVITIES

Section 1: The Earth in Model Form — the Globe

1. Demonstrate to the class how the sun shines on the globe by turning out the classroom lights and shining a flashlight on the globe from the different angles. This illustration could lead into a discussion of the light side of the earth versus the dark side of the earth, the causes of seasons, and so on.

2. Have the students, one-by-one, find the cities of your choice on the globe. Have them approximate mileage from your present location to that particular city. It would also be beneficial for the students to surmise the topography surrounding that city, its climate, and other pertinent facts as revealed by the globe.

3. Divide the class into small groups and assign a country to each group. Have the group elect a chairperson and a secretary or recorder. Challenge the group to find all they can about the country using just the globe as a reference tool. Allow the groups to report to the class on their findings.

4. Have each member of the class research an occupation in which global information would be used regularly. Have students discuss the occupations.

5. Have students find at least one person outside the classroom and explain to that person the significance of the globe. Encourage the students to report to the teacher or the class on their results.

6. Have students research a person whose study of, use of, or theories about the shape of the world or the globe have been significant in providing us knowledge and information. Assign them to write a report from their research.

Section 2: The Earth in Picture Form — the Map

1. Invite a speaker to the class to speak on "The Value of Cartography in Today's World." The speaker could be anyone well-versed in the production of maps.

2. Show a video on map production.

3. Divide the class into small groups and instruct each group to design a realistic map of their choice. The map must include all elements of a well-designed map. Allow the students time to survey the area to be mapped (campus, classroom, administration building). Care must be taken by the groups to draw the map to scale and to include a key or legend. Once the maps have been carefully drawn, students should review each other's work.

4. As a class, gather samples of maps used by people in specific fields—surveyors, pilots, prospectors, hikers, cross-country skiers, sailors, geologists—make a room display of the map samples.

5. Have students map their own neighborhood. Encourage them to be creative in this venture by choosing a specific type of map to draw—topographic, pictorial, and so on. Display the appropriate maps.

6. Assign students to write a paper on the subject, "The Map is Not the Territory."

Section 3: The Earth in Symbol Form — Graphs and Charts

1. Divide the class into small groups and assign each group the task of graphing some aspect of the classroom. The graphs could be an organization of shoe sizes represented by students, styles of automobiles driven by students' parents, types of pets owned by students. Allow each group time to present its chart or graph to the rest of the class.

2. Prepare a display of graphs, charts, and geographic source material for students to peruse at their leisure.

3. Take a trip to the library. Have the librarian explain the geographical material that can be found there.

4. Invite a resource speaker to your classroom to present the effective use of charts, graphs, and geographical material in various fields.

5. Have students make a chart or graph of some aspect of home life. The chart or graph might reflect types of shrubs surrounding your home, the number of relatives in your family and their present geographic location, or anything else that could be reflected in a chart. If you desire, display work in the classroom.

6. Instruct students to use one of the geographic sources in the library to find information about the geography of their state or another state. Assign students to make an oral report to the class on their findings.

Administer the LIFEPAC Test

The test is to be administered in one session. Give no help except with directions.
Evaluate the tests and review areas where the students have done poorly.
Review the pages and activities that stress the concepts tested.
If necessary, administer the Alternate LIFEPAC Test.

ANSWER KEYS

SECTION 1

1.1	true		**1.36**	true
1.2	false		**1.37**	false
1.3	false		**1.38**	true
1.4	true		**1.39**	true
1.5	true		**1.40**	false
1.6	Greeks		**1.41**	true
1.7	150 B.C.		**1.42**	true

1.8 Either order:
a. the Americas
b. Australia

1.9 political
1.10 color
1.11 c
1.12 b
1.13 d
1.14 a
1.15 two: top and bottom
1.16 Examples:
changes in temperature
changes in seasons
changes in lengths of day and night
changes in travel
changes in dress
1.17 false
1.18 false
1.19 true
1.20 true
1.21 false
1.22 true
1.23 false
1.24 false
1.25 false
1.26 If fall or winter is approaching, the hours should decrease. If spring or summer is approaching, the hours should increase.
1.27 a. west
b. east
1.28 axis
1.29 sun
1.30 Either order:
a. tilting
b. revolution
1.31 a
1.32 c
1.33 b
1.34 d
1.35 b

1.43 false
1.44 false
1.45 distortion
1.46 projection
1.47 Mercator
1.48 azimuthal equidistant projection
1.49 equator
1.50 two
1.51 interrupted-area projection
1.52 d
1.53 a
1.54 c
1.55 Teacher check
1.56 53
1.57 15
1.58 6
1.59 Either order:
a. latitude
b. longitude
1.60 4
1.61 true
1.62 false
1.63 false
1.64 false
1.65 Either order:
a. the latitude at which the sun will be directly overhead at noon on specific dates
b. the difference between clock time and sun time
1.66 about seven minutes
1.67 fast

SELF TEST 1

1.01 twenty-four hours
1.02 globe
1.03 Greeks
1.04 Any order:
  a. northern
  b. southern
  c. eastern
  d. western
1.05 a. west
  b. east
1.06 Any order:
  a. Mercator projection
  b. azimuthal equidistant projection
  c. interrupted-area projection
1.07 Either order:
  a. latitude
  b. longitude
1.08 a. Eastern
  b. Central
  c. Mountain
  d. Pacific
1.09 d
1.010 e
1.011 c
1.012 a
1.013 f
1.014 h
1.015 i
1.016 g
1.017 b
1.018 k
1.019 true
1.020 false
1.021 false
1.022 true
1.023 false
1.024 false
1.025 false
1.026 b
1.027 d
1.028 c
1.029 d
1.030 a
1.031 Either order:
  a. the latitude at which the sun will be directly overhead at noon on specific dates
  b. the difference between clock time and sun time

SECTION 2

2.1 b
2.2 c
2.3 a
2.4 d
2.5 c
2.6 a
2.7 Answer could include circles, arrows, shading, and so forth.
2.8 Answer should mention something about going from the concrete to the abstract.
2.9 false
2.10 true
2.11 false
2.12 true
2.13 a. 20 inches
  b. 30 inches
  c. 12 inches to 1 inch
     actual size   scale drawing
  d. 12 inches to 1/2 inch
     actual size   scale drawing
2.14 250
2.15 350
2.16 100 people
2.17 700 people
2.18 State E
2.19 30,000 people
2.20 A = 29 dots
  B =   7 dots
  C = 23 dots
  D = 32 dots
  E =   6 dots
2.21 23
2.22 State E
2.23 false
2.24 true
2.25 true
2.26 false
2.27 Texas
2.28 Florida *or* Michigan
2.29 western
2.30 3
2.31 false
2.32 false
2.33 true
2.34 true
2.35 Teacher check
2.36 They merely give an idea and, thus, do not need to be precisely accurate.

2.37 Examples:
Giving directions to a location, remembering how to find a favorite geographic spot, helping to understand a location, and illustrating an explanation of where you live.

2.38 Hint:
Consult your state's road map.

2.39 Hint:
The student must either use their own scale of miles to measure the route or add the mileage listed on the map between towns along the route.

2.40 They do not understand the symbols on the map.

2.41 Hint:
Answer should include a greater "feel" for the landforms.

2.42 true
2.43 true
2.44 false
2.45 true
2.46 false
2.47 false
2.48 b
2.49 b
2.50 a
2.51 d
2.52 c
2.53 Examples:
a. California
b. water rights, common borders, etc.
c. common needs, trade, etc.
2.54 a. 30°
b. south
c. 15°
d. west
e. 30° south, 15° west

SELF TEST 2

2.01 c
2.02 e
2.03 f
2.04 b
2.05 d
2.06 a
2.07 g
2.08 b
2.09 c
2.010 a
2.011 d
2.012 a
2.013 c
2.014 d
2.015 d
2.016 b
2.017 a
2.018 key *or* legend
2.019 distorted
2.020 map
2.021 projection
2.022 scales or miles
2.023 relief
2.024 parallel
2.025 waterfall
2.026 windbreak
or barrier; boundary
2.027 topographic
2.028 true
2.029 true
2.030 true
2.031 false
2.032 false
2.033 false
2.034 false
2.035 true
2.036 true
2.037 Latitude: 18° south
Longitude: 178° east
2.038 950,000
2.039 210 miles

SECTION 3

3.1	true
3.2	false
3.3	false
3.4	true
3.5	false
3.6	a
3.7	d
3.8	c
3.9	b
3.10	Population in millions
3.11	about 137 million
3.12	about 30 million
3.13	1880
3.14	yes
3.15	15%
3.16	sugar
3.17	true
3.18	true
3.19	false
3.20	false
3.21	true

3.22 Any order:
 a. pictographs
 b. broken bar graphs
 c. bar graph
 d. line graph
 e. circle graph

3.23 Any order:
 a. relationship charts
 b. flow charts
 c. summarization charts

3.24 relationship chart

3.25 flow chart

3.26 Either order:
 a. the organization of information
 b. the clarification of understanding

3.27 a. Name one of the three basic types of charts: relationship, flow, *or* summarization.
 b. Answer could include it: simplifies, clarifies, attracts, organizes, and so forth.

3.28 Any order:
 a. encyclopedia
 b. dictionary
 c. atlas
 or *Statistical Abstract of the United States;*
  The Commodity Yearbook;
  The Agricultural Yearbook;
  The World Almanac;
  The South American Handbook;
  The Statesman's Yearbook;
  The Statistical Yearbook of the United Nations

3.29 atlas

3.30 encyclopedia

3.31 reference materials

SELF TEST 3

3.01	visual
3.02	encyclopedia
3.03	line
3.04	circle
3.05	zero
3.06	atlas
3.07	relationship
3.08	flow
3.09	symbols *or* pictures
3.010	comparison
3.011	d
3.012	j
3.013	g
3.014	c
3.015	a
3.016	e
3.017	i
3.018	h
3.019	k
3.020	b
3.021	b
3.022	c
3.023	b
3.024	d
3.025	a
3.026	f
3.027	c
3.028	c
3.029	d
3.030	a
3.031	false
3.032	true
3.033	false
3.034	false
3.035	true
3.036	true
3.037	true
3.038	true
3.039	true
3.040	false
3.041	Any order: pictograph, broken bar graph, bar graph, line graph, and circle graph
3.042	Either order: the organization of information and the clarification of understanding
3.043	The parts do not equal 100 percent.

3.044 Any order:
an encyclopedia, a dictionary, an atlas, *or*
Statistical Abstract of the United States;
The Commodity Yearbook;
The Agricultural Yearbook;
The Statesman's Yearbook;
The World Almanac;
The South American Handbook;
The Statistical Yearbook of the United Nations

LIFEPAC TEST

1. l
2. h
3. a
4. k
5. f
6. m
7. d
8. c
9. j
10. b
11. g
12. e
13. false
14. true
15. true
16. false
17. false
18. true
19. true
20. true
21. true
22. false
23. distorted
24. projection
25. encyclopedia
26. atlas
27. library
28. meridian
   or longitudinal line
29. parallel
30. key
31. twenty-four hours
32. year
   or 365 1/4 days
33. Either order:
   a. latitude
      or parallel
   b. longitude
      or meridian
34. c
35. a
36. b
37. c
38. b
39. b
40. d
41. It shows the latitude at which the sun will be directly overhead at noon on specific dates.
42. 43° North, 88° West
43. 160 miles

ALTERNATE LIFEPAC TEST

1. twenty-four hours
2. globe
3. analemma
4. key or legend
5. geographer
6. relief
7. parallel
8. visual
9. k
10. g
11. j
12. f
13. h
14. e
15. a
16. b
17. c
18. i
19. true
20. false
21. false
22. true
23. true
24. false
25. true
26. b
27. c
28. a
29. d
30. c
31. b
32. a
33. Any order:
   a. relationship charts
   b. flow charts
   c. summarization charts

HISTORY & GEOGRAPHY 909

ALTERNATE LIFEPAC TEST

NAME _____

DATE _____

SCORE _____

59

74

Complete these sentences (each answer, 3 points).

1. The earth rotates once every _____ .

2. The most accurate representation of the earth's surface is the _____ .

3. A tool found on the globe which helps to determine sun time is the _____ .

4. A map's symbols are explained in its _____ .

5. A map is an important tool of the _____ .

6. A map that you can make with a raised surface is a _____ map.

7. Another name for a latitudinal line is a(n) _____ .

8. Graphs and charts are a form of _____ aid.

Match these items (each answer, 2 points).

9.	_____ intersect	a.	orbit
10.	_____ book of maps	b.	relationship
11.	_____ hemisphere	c.	equator
12.	_____ type of chart	d.	highways
13.	_____ statistics	e.	library reference file
14.	_____ card catalog	f.	summarization
15.	_____ revolution	g.	atlas
16.	_____ most effective chart	h.	numerical facts
17.	_____ great circle route	i.	organize
18.	_____ purpose of a chart	j.	half of earth
		k.	to cross each other

Answer _true_ **or** _false_ (each answer, 1 point).

19. _____ It takes 365 days for the earth to orbit around the sun.

20. _____ Great circle routes are no longer used for travel.

21. _____ The analemma is used to determine how far a country is located from the equator.

22. _____ You may see a corn stalk on a pictorial map of Nebraska.

23. _____ An outline map requires you to fill in details.

24. _____ _The Statesman's Yearbook_ is not a geographic resource book.

25. _____ A helpful tool for locating magazine articles is the _Readers' Guide to Periodical Literature_.

Write the letter for the correct answer on each line (each answer, 2 points).

26. A scale of miles helps to measure distances on a _____ .
   a. chart   b. map
   c. graph   d. geographer

27. Latitude and longitude help to _____ positions on a map.
   a. measure   b. change
   c. locate   d. charge

28. The earth can be divided into _____ hemispheres.
   a. 4   b. 0
   c. 3   d. 16

29. Meridians are lines that run _____ .
   a. in and out   b. east and west
   c. around and under   d. north and south

30. Oceans are a natural _____ .
   a. bridge   b. disaster
   c. barrier   d. nuisance

31. The value of a graph is determined by its _____ .
   a. color   b. usefulness
   c. size   d. weight

32. "Greenwich" is a _____ .
   a. town   b. watch
   c. mountain   d. sandwich

Complete this sentence (each answer, 3 points).

33. The three major types of charts are a. _____ ,

    b. _____ , and c. _____ .

HISTORY & GEOGRAPHY 910

Unit 10: Man in a Changing World

TEACHER NOTES

MATERIALS NEEDED FOR LIFEPAC	
Required	Suggested
None	• encyclopedia or reference books for research • dictionary • maps of the world • sample charts and graphs • Bible • reference books or online sources

ADDITIONAL LEARNING ACTIVITIES

Section 1: Historical Background of the United States

1. With the assistance of the students, list on a chart or chalkboard a chronology of the important events in the settlement and expansion of the United States. Allow the chronology to remain visible until the LIFEPAC is completed.

2. Lead a review game on the settlement and expansion of the United States, United States government, and the major changes in America over the years. Students might be divided into teams for this question and answer game.

3. Arrange a visit to a city council meeting or the meeting of one of the county commissions. If you live in or near a state capital, you might attend a legislative session or committee session. When you return, discuss what was observed.

4. Arrange a visit to a museum, library, or other place that contains historical displays on the United States.

5. Assign students to write a comparison/contrast paper: Explore the similarities and differences in United States government and living conditions between the past and today.

6. Have students use what they know about America's history and current events in order to predict what will happen to America in the next twenty years. Have students report to the class and discuss.

Section 2: Development of Earth

1. Compile a series of newspaper, magazine articles, pictures, books, or online resources on early geography and regions of the earth. Have a class discussion on the influence of these conditions on the culture and life styles of the people.

2. Gather as many tools of geography as you can. Display these items or pictures of them during the LIFEPAC study.

3. Have the class dramatize the beginning of the earth for the rest of the school or for parents.

4. Have a group discussion of all the ways your life would be different if you were from another region. Then, choose a different region to use in your discussion.

5. Have students explain, in their own words, the beginning of the earth to a person who is younger than you are.

6. Assign students to read a book about a person who lives in another geographical region of the world, and then make a report to contrast lifestyles between regions.

Section 3: Commitment to the Future

1. Help students organize an environmental campaign. Bring newspapers and magazines to class or suggest online resources to help students in this project. Books and other articles on ecology will be helpful, too. The campaign might center on a local problem or might be one of national interest.
    Brainstorm with students to get ideas. Help students decide how they might attack the problem by letter writing or doing the work themselves (in the case of a park that needs cleaning). Later, have a discussion on the process and its success or failure.

2. Have individual conferences with students on career choices and life planning. If interest inventories are available to you, use them to help students determine where their strengths and weaknesses lie.

3. Plan a career day. Invite people from colleges and industries to be available during the day to answer career and lifestyle questions. Or you might prefer to invite people who have different careers to speak to your class once a week during your study of this LIFEPAC.

4. Invite a person who has served on a jury to speak to your class about their experience as a juror.

5. Have students visit someone who is in a career field they are interested in or whose lifestyle they admire. Instruct students to find out as much relevant information as possible about the career or lifestyle. Then, assign students to write a report telling why their career or lifestyle decision remains the same or is changed after the experience.

6. Provide the following instructions for a project: Survey your community to decide what is, in your opinion, the most serious environmental problem. Decide how you as a citizen can help solve the problem. Then follow through by writing letters, talking with a government official, or doing any other work you think you must do to help solve the problem.

Administer the LIFEPAC Test

The test is to be administered in one session. Give no help except with directions.
Evaluate the tests and review areas where the students have done poorly.
Review the pages and activities that stress the concepts tested.
If necessary, administer the Alternate LIFEPAC Test.

ANSWER KEYS

SECTION 1

1.1 Either order:
  a. religious
  b. political
1.2 Any order:
  a. diligence
  b. stewardship
  c. courage
  d. faith
  e. single-mindedness
1.3 Any order:
  a. freedom of speech
  b. freedom of religion
  c. freedom from want
  d. freedom from fear
1.4 a. 1492
  b. Columbus discovered West Indies
1.5 French
1.6 c
1.7 b, d, e, f, and c
1.8 b
1.9 c
1.10 b
1.11 a
1.12 c
1.13 a
1.14 Any order:
  a. from different countries
  b. different languages
  c. different classes of society
  d. different religions
  e. lived far apart
1.15 Any order:
  a. all spoke English
  b. fought together
  c. lived alike
  d. same problems
  e. all part of Britain
1.16 a. Revolutionary
  b. 1783
1.17 Either order:
  a. taxation without representation
  b. acts were passed that restricted them in all areas of life
1.18 Either order:
  a. maintain independence
  b. protect rights as free men

1.19 b
  d
  a
  c
1.20 slaves provided labor force to produce crops of cotton, sugar, tobacco, rice
1.21 a. slavery
  b. union
1.22 Teacher check
1.23 b
  d
  e
  a
  c
1.24 a. 6
  b. 3
  c. 1
  d. 4
  e. 5
  f. 2
1.25 after the Spanish American War in 1898
1.26 Any order:
  a. land
  b. wealth
  c. adventure
1.27 the governed – the people
1.28 life, liberty, and the pursuit of happiness
1.29 1788
1.30 Any order:
  a. to form a more perfect Union
  b. to establish justice or equality under the law
  c. to insure domestic tranquility – peace
  d. to provide for common defense
  e. to promote general welfare of citizens
  f. to secure the blessings of liberty
1.31 gives basic plan and structure of government; states relationship between states and federal government; outlines process for making amendments and ratification
1.32 by amendments
1.33 Any order:
  a. executive
  b. legislative
  c. judicial
1.34 legislative branch
1.35 executive branch
1.36 judicial branch

1.37 no one leader or small group of men could take over power

1.38 democracy

1.39 Any order:
a. protection
b. welfare
c. transportation
d. safety

1.40 a group of people occupying a definite territory, under one government, not subject to outside control

1.41 Any order:
a. collect taxes
b. establish courts
c. borrow money
d. enforce laws
e. punish lawbreakers
f. provide for people's health and welfare

1.42 Either order:
a. federal
b. state

1.43 state

1.44 a. Jamestown, Virginia
b. council
c. John Smith

1.45 a. work
b. eat

1.46 if any would not work, neither should he eat

1.47 Any order:
a. collects taxes
b. supervises elections
c. sees that state laws are carried out

1.48 Any order:
a. roads
b. public education
c. zoning
d. licensing

1.49 Any order:
a. health
b. education
c. safety

1.50 Any order:
a. Mayor-Council Plan
b. Commission Plan
c. City Manager Plan

1.51 b
d
e
g
h
f
c
a

1.52 Any order:
a. steam
b. petroleum
c. electricity

1.53 Any order:
a. business enterprises
b. better production
c. financing

1.54 a. communication
b. transportation
c. electricity
d. medicine
e. trades

1.55 emphasized family; other things become more important

1.56 specialization rather than self-sufficiency

1.57 Any order:
a. tide of immigrants
b. high productivity
c. the highest standard of living in the world
d. people moved from farms to cities
e. decentralized families

1.58 humanism

1.59 Either order:
a. East
b. Midwest

1.60 League of Nations

1.61 God

1.62 c

1.63 d

1.64 b

1.65 court decision

1.66 to teach children how to read in order to read Bible

1.67 Either order:
a. Bible reading
b. prayer

1.68 Any order:
a. rights of voters
b. rights of employment
c. right of public accommodation

1.69 Any order:
a. takes human lives
b. drains a nation's health and productivity
c. wastes the land and its natural resources

1.70 false

1.71 true

1.72 false

1.73 false

1.74 true

1.75 true

1.76 e

1.77 c

1.78 h

1.79 a
1.80 k
1.81 g
1.82 i
1.83 d
1.84 b
1.85 j
1.86 Either order:
    a. to help man find raw materials
    b. to discover new and better methods of productivity
1.87 canals
1.88 Either order:
    a. Panama
    b. Suez
1.89 Either order:
    a. diesel
    b. nuclear power
1.90 open pit
1.91 Any order:
    a. geologists
    b. chemists
    c. geophysicists
1.92 using scientific knowledge
1.93 true
1.94 false
1.95 false
1.96 false
1.97 true
1.98 false
1.99 true
1.100 false
1.101 true
1.102 false
1.103 true
1.104 true

SELF TEST 1

1.01 d
1.02 k
1.03 a
1.04 c
1.05 g
1.06 b
1.07 h
1.08 f
1.09 j
1.010 i
1.011 a
1.012 c
1.013 b
1.014 b
1.015 c
1.016 b
1.017 a
1.018 Any order:
    a. political freedom
    b. religious freedom
    c. wealth
    d. power
    or adventure, a "second chance" for a new life
1.019 Any order:
    a. land
    b. wealth
    c. adventure
1.020 Any order:
    a. executive
    b. legislative
    c. judicial
1.021 Any order:
    a. soil
    b. water
    c. minerals
    or gold, oil, coal, silver, iron ore
1.022 Any order:
    a. steam
    b. petroleum
    c. electricity
1.023 Any order:
    a. people moved from farms to cities
    b. increase in size and number of cities
    c. decentralized families
1.024 false
1.025 false
1.026 false
1.027 true
1.028 false
1.029 true
1.030 true

1.031 true
1.032 true
1.033 false
1.034 true
1.035 true
1.036 e
1.037 g
1.038 h
1.039 i
1.040 c
1.041 d
1.042 a
1.043 j
1.044 b
1.045 f

SECTION 2

2.1 true
2.2 false
2.3 false
2.4 true
2.5 false
2.6 true
2.7 false
2.8 true
2.9 true
2.10 false
2.11 Noah was a godly man who found grace in the eyes of the Lord
2.12 forty
2.13 underground rivers
2.14 Ararat
2.15 fossil fuel
2.16 strata
2.17 Adam
2.18 Any order:
a. built cities
b. enjoyed music
c. worked with metals
d. code of law and justice
2.19 a. common
b. disobedience
2.20 civilization
2.21 Babel
2.22 migrated
2.23 Teacher check
2.24 b
c
a
2.25 cuneiform
2.26 Any order:
a. great leaders
b. military campaigns
c. religious music
d. records of Sumerian laws
2.27 Mesopotamia
2.28 hieroglyphics
2.29 Either order:
a. Tigris
b. Euphrates
2.30 Hammurabi
2.31 pharaohs
2.32 a. traders
b. alphabet
2.33 a. father
b. Hebrew
2.34 discovered that the raising of livestock and crops would provide a stable, adequate food supply

2.35 Any order:
  a. tools
  b. weapons
  c. mediums of exchange (money)

2.36 Any order:
  a. the Nile area of Egypt
  b. the Mesopotamian area
  c. the Indus valley
  d. the Hwang Ho valley of China

2.37 Any order:
  a. worship of the true and living God
  b. the Bible
  c. basic religious concepts used today

2.38 c
  e
  b
  c
  f
  a
  a
  e
  d
  f
  g
  h
  h
  c

2.39 inland

2.40 a. alphabet
  b. Phoenicians

2.41 Either order:
  a. history
  b. science

2.42 Any order:
  a. Etruscans
  b. Greeks
  c. Egyptians

2.43 Any order:
  a. system of coded laws
  b. Latin
  c. paved roads and aqueducts

2.44 b
  d
  b
  a
  c
  d
  b
  c
  b

2.45 desert

2.46 Any order:
  a. Nubia
  b. Mali
  c. Kush
  d. Bantu
  e. Aksum
  or Lubas, Ghana, Songhai, Kongo

2.47 Kongo

2.48 false

2.49 false

2.50 true

2.51 false

2.52 a

2.53 b

2.54 c

2.55 c

2.56 a

2.57 b

2.58 b

2.59 a

2.60 c

2.61 navigation

2.62 Mediterranean Sea

2.63 Phoenicia

2.64 Either order:
  a. King David
  b. Solomon

2.65 Chinese

2.66 Leif Erickson

2.67 Either order:
  a. Panama
  b. Suez

2.68 inland

2.69 Either order:
  a. diesel fuel
  b. nuclear power

2.70 Either order:
  a. sails
  b. oars

2.71 d

2.72 b

2.73 b

2.74 c

2.75 d

2.76 a

2.77 Any order:
  a. the availability of jobs
  b. easier access to religious, cultural, and recreational activities
  c. seeking a better way of life

2.78 Any order:
  a. by canal
  b. by turnpike
  c. by railroad

2.79 Either order:
a. enable man to find the raw materials in the earth
b. develop better ways to use resources

2.80 Any order:
a. manufacturing
b. transportation
c. communication
d. medicine
e. the arts
f. business and finance
g. use of leisure time

2.81 spheric (circular)

2.82 distort

2.83 rotation

2.84 a. revolution
b. sun

2.85 Either order:
a. land
b. water

2.86 true

2.87 true

2.88 false

2.89 false

2.90 false

2.91 false

2.92 true

2.93 gravity

2.94 space travel

2.95 Any order:
a. patterns of flight
b. atmospheric conditions
c. distance

2.96 Either order:
a. amount of artificial light used
b. amount and type of clothing

2.97 Any order:
a. northeast
b. southern
c. western
d. Pacific Coastal

2.98 an area of the world where a certain characteristic is common to the people who live there

2.99 Any order:
a. geographic
b. climactic
c. racial
d. religious
e. political
f. economic

2.100 b

2.101 c

2.102 d

2.103 a

2.104 Any order:
a. Europe
b. Asia
c. Africa
d. North America
e. South America
f. Australia
g. Antarctica

2.105 Any order:
a. White
b. Black or African American
c. American Indian or Alaska Native
d. Asian
e. Native Hawaiian or Other Pacific Islander

2.106 Any order:
a. Christianity
b. Islam
c. Hinduism
d. Confucianism
e. Buddhism
or Shinto, Taoism, and Judaism

2.107 Any order:
a. Free World Bloc
b. Communist Bloc
c. Third World Bloc

2.108 collapse

2.109 European Union

2.110 United States-Mexico-Canada Agreement (USMCA)

2.111 false

2.112 true

2.113 false

2.114 true

2.115 true

2.116 true

SELF TEST 2

2.01 d
2.02 f
2.03 a
2.04 h
2.05 c
2.06 b
2.07 i
2.08 j
2.09 g
2.010 e
2.011 Any order:
    a. increase in size and numbers of cities
    b. changed from agricultural to industrial nation
    c. decentralized families
2.012 Any order:
    a. religious freedom
    b. political freedom
    c. wealth
    d. power
    e. adventure
2.013 Noah was a godly man who found grace in the eyes of the Lord
2.014 disobedience
2.015 a. Tigris
    b. Euphrates
2.016 Any order:
    a. tools
    b. weapons
    c. coins of exchange (money)
2.017 Any order:
    a. worship God
    b. Bible
    c. religious concepts
2.018 Either order:
    a. history
    b. science
2.019 Any order:
    a. system of coded laws
    b. Latin
    c. paved roads and aqueducts
2.020 false
2.021 true
2.022 false
2.023 true
2.024 false
2.025 false
2.026 true
2.027 false
2.028 true
2.029 false

2.030 c
2.031 a
2.032 d
2.033 a
2.034 a
2.035 c
2.036 d
2.037 a
2.038 to enable man to find the raw materials in the earth and to develop better ways to use resources
2.039 Any order:
    a. the Free World Bloc
    b. the Communist Bloc
    c. the Third World Bloc
2.040 The collapse of the USSR ended the military power that supported communism worldwide. This ended the major threat of communism and the three-bloc system set up because of that threat.
2.041 b
2.042 d
2.043 e
2.044 a
2.045 f
2.046 c
2.047 g
2.048 j
2.049 h
2.050 i

SECTION 3

3.1 during the time in the garden of Eden
3.2 Either order:
    a. increased in numbers
    b. became technologically advanced
3.3 Either order:
    a. conservation
    b. restoration
3.4 God
3.5 Either order:
    a. choose a type of work that relates to environment
    b. practice conservation in daily living
3.6 c
3.7 f
3.8 d
3.9 b
3.10 e
3.11 a
3.12 true
3.13 false
3.14 false
3.15 false
3.16 Any order:
    a. a
    b. c
    c. e
    d. f
3.17 a. b
    b. c
3.18 stress
3.19 respecting
3.20 Any order:
    a. wood products
    b. clean air
    c. recreation
    d. watershed
3.21 Either order:
    a. coal
    b. oil
    c. gas
3.22 nuclear
3.23 Any order:
    a. secular
    b. urbanized
    c. industrial
3.24 free enterprise
3.25 welfare

3.26 Any order:
    a. federal minimum wage
    b. required recruitment of minorities, women, and people with disabilities
    c. filing of government regulatory forms
    d. complex tax system
3.27 true
3.28 true
3.29 false
3.30 true
3.31 false
3.32 true
3.33 false
3.34 true
3.35 b
3.36 Either order:
    a. a
    b. c
3.37 Either order:
    a. b
    b. d
3.38 Either order:
    a. reduced lifestyle
    b. another family member securing a job
3.39 Families buy more things than they can afford because credit is easy to obtain
3.40 Any order:
    a. inflation
    b. layoffs
    c. strikes
    d. poor weather
    e. increased taxes
3.41 false
3.42 true
3.43 false
3.44 true
3.45 false
3.46 false
3.47 false
3.48 true
3.49 Either order:
    a. work
    b. family relationships
3.50 family
3.51 culture
3.52 a. church
    b. family
3.53 Either order:
    a. pleasing God
    b. financial independence
3.54 husband
3.55 stress
3.56 Bible

3.57   b, c, d
3.58   true
3.59   true
3.60   false
3.61   20,000
3.62   diversity
3.63   specialization
3.64   true
3.65   false
3.66   false
3.67   true
3.68   true
3.69   false
3.70   false
3.71   a. ___S___
        b. ___P___
        c. __S-P__
        d. __S-P__
        e. ___S___
        f. ___P___
        g. ___S___
        h. ___P___
3.72   a. lamp
        b. light
3.73   a. ear
        b. heart
3.74   a. God
        b. wisdom
        c. Bible
        d. decisions
        e. glory
3.75   Any order:
        a. what the Bible says (conscience)
        b. how a person feels (desire)
        c. inner peace (calm and rightness)
        d. one's ability with God's power (freedom)
        e. circumstances (open and closed doors)
3.76   a, b, e
3.77   Teacher check
3.78   true
3.79   false
3.80   true
3.81   false
3.82   false
3.83   true
3.84   false
3.85   true
3.86   false
3.87   false
3.88   true

3.89   personal rights
3.90   procedural
3.91   Either order:
        a. substantive
        b. procedural
3.92   First
3.93   false
3.94   false
3.95   true
3.96   false
3.97   false
3.98   true
3.99   true
3.100   Any order:
        a. indictment by a grand jury
        b. protection against double jeopardy
        c. assurance against self-incrimination
        d. provision for the due process of law
3.101   government
3.102   a. immunities
        b. citizens
3.103   representatives
3.104   Any order:
        a. letters
        b. personal interviews
        c. assemblies
        or marches, demonstrations
3.105   Either order:
        a. Democratic
        b. Republican
3.106   Teacher check
3.107   false
3.108   true
3.109   false

SELF TEST 3

3.01   d
3.02   g
3.03   h
3.04   i
3.05   j
3.06   e
3.07   a
3.08   b
3.09   c
3.010 f
3.011 a
3.012 c
3.013 b
3.014 d
3.015 a
3.016 c
3.017 a
3.018 true
3.019 false
3.020 true
3.021 true
3.022 false
3.023 true
3.024 true
3.025 true
3.026 true
3.027 false
3.028 ecology
3.029 Either order:
    a. animals
    b. humans
3.030 government
3.031 peace
3.032 family
3.033 Bible
3.034 Any order:
    a. service
    b. dedication
    c. achievement
3.035 2
3.036 3
3.037 5
2.038 4
2.039 1
3.040 7
3.041 6

3.042 Any order:
    a. Free World Bloc
    b. Communist Bloc
    c. Third World Bloc
3.043 Any order:
    a. wood products
    b. clean air
    c. recreation
    d. watershed
3.044 Any order:
    a. inflation
    b. layoffs
    c. strikes
    d. poor weather
    e. increased taxes
3.045 Any order:
    a. what the Bible says
    b. how a person feels
    c. inner peace
    d. one's ability with God's power
    e. circumstances
3.046 false
3.047 false
3.048 true
3.049 true
3.050 true
3.051 false
3.052 true
3.053 true

LIFEPAC TEST

1. e
2. g
3. h
4. b
5. d
6. j
7. a
8. c
9. f
10. i
11. true
12. false
13. false
14. true
15. false
16. true
17. true
18. false
19. true
20. false
21. Union
22. John Glenn
23. Rome
24. free enterprise
25. Department of Labor
26. naturalization
27. family
28. career
29. b
30. b
31. a
32. d
33. a
34. c
35. Any order:
    a. b
    b. c
    c. e
36. a
37. Any order:
    a. a
    b. b
    c. d
38. 2
39. 3
40. 5
41. 4
42. 1
43. 7
44. 6

ALTERNATE LIFEPAC TEST

1. g
2. a
3. j
4. d
5. i
6. c
7. b
8. e
9. f
10. h
11. true
12. false
13. false
14. true
15. false
16. true
17. true
18. false
19. false
20. false
21. b
22. c
23. d
24. a
25. b
26. c
27. a
28. b
29. d
30. b
31. amendments
32. Any order
    a. executive
    b. legislative
    c. judicial
33. state
34. Either order:
    a. national guard
    b. taxation
35. city government
36. f
37. c
38. h
39. b
40. d
41. j
42. e
43. g
44. a
45. i

HISTORY & GEOGRAPHY 910

ALTERNATE LIFEPAC TEST

NAME _____

DATE _____

SCORE _____

Match these items (each answer, 2 points).

1. _____ Jamestown
2. _____ Boston Tea Party
3. _____ Appomattox
4. _____ Alaska
5. _____ Nile River
6. _____ Ur
7. _____ Mediterranean Sea
8. _____ Greenwich, England
9. _____ Louisiana Purchase
10. _____ Gadsden Purchase

a. protested taxation without representation
b. largest inland body of water
c. cuneiform tablets
d. purchased from Russia
e. prime meridian
f. land from France in 1803
g. first colony in the New World
h. parts of Arizona and New Mexico
i. Egyptian Civilization
j. South's surrender

Answer *true* **or** *false* (each answer, 2 points).

11. _____ Plants perform a cleansing of the air by absorbing carbon monoxide.
12. _____ A career is merely a job one performs to earn money.
13. _____ Once a person has gained citizenship in the United States, they cannot ever lose it.

14. _____ Jury duty is a duty of citizenship.

15. _____ Security should be the main goal in a Christian's life.

16. _____ The Hindus used a number and decimal system derived from the Arabs.

17. _____ The Aztecs were primarily agriculturalists.

18. _____ The globe is a perfect sphere, the same shape as the earth.

19. _____ The line that separates North Korea and South Korea is the 48th parallel.

20. _____ The climate of a region has very little effect on the culture of that region.

Write the letter for the correct answer on each line (each answer, 2 points).

21. Today, the agricultural loss of farmland has resulted in _____ .
    a. loss of money for producers of farm equipment
    b. ecological problems particularly in air quality
    c. farmers making windfall profits on the sale of land
    d. world hunger

22. Most of the energy in the United States comes from _____ .
    a. nuclear power   b. solar energy
    c. fossil fuels   d. wind and water power

23. A main reason workers are fired is _____ .
    a. they are unskilled at the work they are doing
    b. they are overqualified for the work they are doing
    c. they have been dishonest with or have stolen something from their employer
    d. they cannot get along with other people

24. Procedural rights of a citizen protect _____ .
    a. an individual's integrity
    b. an individual's right to worship as they please
    c. an individual's right to express themself
    d. an individual's right to assemble

25. A responsible citizen should act _____ .
    a. out of a sense of obligation
    b. freely and willingly
    c. restrictively
    d. reservedly

26. The best way to increase voter participation in elections is _____ .
    a. to make voter registration as easy as possible
    b. to increase the hours that polling places are open at election time
    c. to educate the citizen in their civic responsibilities
    d. to provide free transportation to the polling places

27. The English colonists settled primarily _____ .
    a. along the Atlantic coast
    b. inland in areas that are now Ohio, West Virginia, and Indiana
    c. along the Mississippi
    d. west of the Appalachian Mountains

28. One result of the Civil War was _____ .
    a. Abraham Lincoln became president of the United States
    b. the slaves were freed
    c. the army of Ulysses S. Grant was defeated
    d. people in the Southern states changed their minds about slavery

29. After the _____ the United States was recognized as a world power.
    a. War of 1812   b. Revolutionary War
    c. Civil War   d. Spanish-American War

30. The United States government received its authority to govern from _____ .
    a. God   b. the people
    c. the Congress   d. the Constitution

Complete these sentences (each answer, 3 points).

31. The last section of the Constitution consists of the _____ .

32. The three branches of the federal government are a. _____ ,

    b. _____ , and c. _____ .

33. Education is one of the rights left to the _____ by the federal government.

34. Two shared powers of the federal and state governments are a. _____

    and b. _____ .

35. The most important unit of local government in the United States is

    _____ .

Match these items (each answer, 2 points).

36. _____ Daniel Jackling

37. _____ Noah

38. _____ Richard Nixon

39. _____ Woodrow Wilson

40. _____ George Westinghouse

41. _____ Moses

42. _____ Hammurabi

43. _____ Chin Dynasty

44. _____ Charles Goodyear

45. _____ naturalization

a. vulcanization of rubber

b. League of Nations

c. universal Flood

d. automatic air brake

e. universal code of law

f. open-pit mining

g. the Great Wall

h. Watergate

i. the process for an immigrant to become a citize

j. led Hebrews out of Egyptian bondage